B11189

BBC MUSIC GUIDES

Bach Organ Music

PETER WILLIAMS

BRITISH BROADCASTING CORPORATION

Contents

Published by the British Broadcasting Corporation
35 Marylebone High Street, London W1M 4AA

ISBN 0 563 10348 5
First published 1972
Reprinted 1974, 1977, 1980, 1983
© Peter Williams 1972

Printed in England by Spottiswoode Ballantyne Ltd
Colchester and London

Introduction

The collection of Bach's organ music entitled *Clavierübung III* contains a group of so-called preludes (*Vorspiele*) based on chorale melodies, each of which is set twice or three times as separate organ pieces. Those on 'Vater unser im Himmelreich' begin as follows:

Ex. 1

(a) BWV 682

(b) BWV 683

There is much to ask or say about such pieces: when they were written, where they come in the composer's development, whether this is their final version, whether they were influenced by other composers' work (there is a florid or coloratura setting of the same melody by Böhm, who may have been Bach's teacher); what their purpose was, whether the source is a good one, whether (since *Clavierübung III* was published) the piece was well known and by whom, why Bach published no organ music before this (he was then 54); what kind of organ they were written for, how they were registered and played; what significance the melody had then or later (is our approach coloured by Mendelssohn's use of the theme?); what meaning the hymn-text had, whether the collection of pieces followed a plan. Such matters are all factual and objective. Even more difficult are the subjective questions, such as 'What is the meaning of such pieces?', while virtually unanswerable are the speculative questions, such as 'Did he employ number or letter symbolism, musical acrostics, recurrent or associative motifs?' We can easily ask questions that the composer himself could not have answered. Yet the most striking thing about Ex. 1 is none of these things: it is a matter of musical observation, and whether we can see signs of a musical ability of such immensity that all other questions remain subsidiary.

The most striking thing is this: the invention that can enable a composer to work from a well-known theme two pieces of completely different musical content, each fully mature and confident, each pushing its character to a kind of limit. The genre is the same: they are both organ chorales, and the theme is ultimately – though not easily – recognisable in both. But the musicianship that can work from one theme both a little fluent 24-bar prelude and an immense piece of over 90 taut, chromatic, involved bars is what must always arouse the greatest attention and admiration. The more complex version is in fact very hard to perform convincingly and could well give the listener ideas on mature composers' tendencies towards the abstract. But that too is a subsidiary matter and must not deflect our admiration for the variety of techniques mastered by a composer commonly regarded today as 'the culmination of an era'.

Early Years

By the age of 18, J. S. Bach was ready for his first post as independent organist; six or seven years later he was sufficiently known as an expert on organ-building to advise on an important three-manual organ in a church of some significance at Mühlhausen. Yet nobody knows for certain how he acquired these skills as player and expert. His early biographers Walther and Forkel[1] say he learnt the organ or *clavier* from his brother Johann

[1] J. G. Walther, *Musicalisches Lexicon* (Leipzig, 1732), under 'Bach, Joh.

Christoph, which is likely; but no evidence has come to light. Like all the musicians of the period, he must have copied a lot of music, and the Obituary Notice[1] mentions his brother's notebook containing pieces by Froberger, Kerl and Pachelbel, but nothing has come down to show the young composer specifically imitating Pachelbel in this early period, however likely it may have been. At Lüneburg J. S. Bach was known as a talented singer and an intelligent schoolboy, but there is no proof, as is commonly supposed, that he studied organ there (in another church of the town) with Georg Böhm. The authenticity of the partitas, said to be written in imitation of Böhm, is still controversial, and even C. P. E. Bach claims only that his father 'loved and studied' Böhm's music, not that he was a pupil.[2] Nothing is known for certain of the supposed early visits to Hamburg to hear Reinken playing in the Katharinenkirche; or whether he still went there after 1702 when Vincent Lübeck became organist of the Nikolaikirche; or whether in or near Lüneburg itself he had any chance to study such famous collections of music as that now called the Lüneburg Organ Tablature (works by Scheidt, Scheidemann, Tunder, Weckmann and others). By the time he went to Lübeck to hear Buxtehude, he was himself a professional organist, apparently risking his post by staying away so long. This post was at Arnstadt, where the Obituary says he 'took the works of Bruhns, Reinken, Buxtehude and several good French organists as models' – such as Nicolas de Grigny, whose *Premier Livre d'Orgue* (1699) he copied a few years later in Weimar. This is one of the best and, in its five-part movements, most carefully written of all the collections of French organ music.

Unprovable by documents though much of this picture is, the whole is most plausible. The composers mentioned represent the best keyboard music of the many countries known collectively as 'Germany', from the southerners Froberger and Kerl to the Hanseatic (and partly Danish) north of Buxtehude and his

Sebastian'; J. N. Forkel, *Über J. S. Bachs Leben, Kunst und Kunstwerke* (Leipzig, 1802), translated in H. T. David & A. Mendel, *The Bach Reader* (New York revised edn. 1966).

[1] Obituary by C. P. E. Bach and J. F. Agricola (1754), translated in David & Mendel, *op cit.*

[2] In a letter to Forkel, C. P. E. Bach actually crossed out the phrase 'his teacher Böhm' and substituted 'the Lüneburg organist Böhm'. See David & Mendel, *op. cit.*, p. 278.

colleagues. To a lively young organist fortunate enough to be brought up in Thuringia – half-way between Munich and Lübeck – the cross-currents must have been able to stimulate intense personal development. There is a remarkable parallel in the case of Gottfried Silbermann, an organ-builder of exactly Bach's period and almost exactly the same area. Certainly Bach had picked up various ideas of *le goût français*, and his own playing retained some French characteristics, judging by Adlung's cryptic remark that he played Louis Marchand's suites 'in his own manner, that is to say, very smoothly and full of artistry'.[1] How much he knew of the French taste before moving to Weimar in 1708 and how much after is an open question; certainly he must have known the older German composers, some personally and many more by their music. J. G. Walther, a distant relation and organist colleague, said he was presented by Bach with two hundred compositions, including works by Böhm and Buxtehude. Throughout his life Bach esteemed many other composers, copying or using their music and even their theory books, though not like Handel directly incorporating their work into his own compositions. The Obituary claimed that by the time of Arnstadt 'he had learned chiefly by the observation of the works of the most famous and proficient composers of his day and by the fruits of his own reflections upon them'. Though the powers 'of his own reflections' were no doubt greater than those of any other composer listed above, this element of self-education in a period full of fine organ music, of incomparable organs and of lively Protestant music-making, is easy to believe in.

Precise influences are difficult to define. Even for an early work like the D major Prelude and Fugue (BWV 532)[2] it would be pointless to remark anything more definite than that there are resemblances to works by both Buxtehude and Pachelbel and that it probably belongs to 'the Arnstadt, Mühlhausen or perhaps early Weimar period'. Nor of course is the music of Bach unusual in having such mixed origins. It is common to assume that his influence on pupils and friends was paramount, but it would be difficult to accredit him with particular details in the music of, say,

[1] Quoted by Spitta, *Johann Sebastian Bach* (English translation, London, 1884), I, p. 585.

[2] *Bach-Werke-Verzeichnis*, a thematic catalogue compiled by Wolfgang Schmieder (Leipzig, 1950).

J. L. Krebs when one of Krebs's manuscripts alone contains works by d'Andrieu, d'Anglebert, Buxtehude, Clérambault, Kauffmann, Lebègue, Lübeck, Marcello, Marchand, Nivers, Telemann, and others. Similarly, one of Walther's manuscript collections included works by many composers beside those of J. S. Bach, for which the collection is famous. C. P. E. Bach noted that in his later years his father admired the music of Fux, Caldara, Handel, Keiser, Hasse, J. G. and K. H. Graun, Telemann, Zelenka and Benda, none of whom was a notable organ-composer; while in his earlier years he had 'heard and studied' Frescobaldi, J. C. F. Fischer, Strunck, 'some old and good Frenchmen', Buxtehude, Reinken, Bruhns, Böhm, as well as Froberger, Kerl and Pachelbel. It is also safe to assume he knew organ music by men he succeeded or nearly succeeded, such as Zachau in Halle and Kuhnau in Leipzig.

It is against the background of this intense musical activity pursued by organists of central Germany that the music of J. S. Bach should be seen. Compared with them, the organists of south and north Germany were mostly provincial and one-sided, to say nothing of other countries like England where even the most widely experienced of organists is unlikely to have known more than a pedal-less piece or two by Kerl or Zipoli.

Organ Chorales in the Service

Unlike many other forms of music, organ music has not only its listeners to satisfy and its composers' musical success to aim at, but the employer, the Church, has certain demands to make of it – it must contribute to the Service. The order of Service varied a great deal, depending, for instance, on the particular shade of Lutheranism adopted by the church concerned. That noted by Bach at Leipzig (Advent, 1723) was:

1 Preluding (i.e. organ voluntary)
2 *Motetta* (motet for choir)
3 Preluding on the Kyrie, which is performed as a piece of concerted music
4 Intoning before the altar
5 Reading of the Epistle
6 Singing of the Litany
7 Preluding on the chorale (i.e. introducing the congregational hymn)

8 Reading of the Gospel
9 Preluding on the principal composition (i.e. introducing the cantata)
10 Singing of the Creed
11 The Sermon
12 Singing of several verses of a hymn
13 Words of Institution (of the Sacrament)
14 Preluding on the composition (i.e. second part of the cantata?)
15 Alternate preluding and singing of chorales until the end of the Communion

Such a scheme reflects an organist's approach to the Service and would be vague to a liturgist; it also described a Service that perhaps changed a little from period to period. But unclear though the details may be, it does show that the organist had more than an incidental part to play, and that he played chiefly in connection with the congregational hymns. It is here, in the organ 'chorale prelude', that the composer probably felt himself to be engaged in his most important activity. According to Adlung,[1] a German organist of about that period and area, there were at least seventeen different techniques for composing (or extemporising) chorale preludes, and they had three purposes:

1 To prepare the congregation for the key
2 To inform them of the tune
3 To delight them 'through fluent ideas' (*durch wohlfliessende Gedanken*)

Many of J. S. Bach's preludes satisfy points 1 and 2 very imperfectly indeed; they seem more to aim at point 3 and even beyond it – at setting a mood, preparing the congregation for the sense and style of the words of the hymn. Whether they prepared them for the correct tune is open to doubt, and practical a composer though Bach was, it is possible that at least some of his organ chorales were written for no utilitarian purpose. Adlung was writing too late and imprecisely to give much idea of how chorale preludes were conceived at Weimar, but many listeners must find it difficult to reconcile the composer's claim that for all music 'the end and purpose should be nothing but the glory of God and the recreation of the spirit' with certain musical intricacies

---

[1] *Anleitung zur musikalischen Gelahrtheit* (1783 edn.), pp. 825 ff.

that might reasonably be assumed to result from regarding music as being for its own sake. But nobody can say. The young Bach criticised at Arnstadt for making 'many curious *variationes* in the chorale' and harmonising the hymns by 'mingling many strange tones in it', or the older Bach weaving an extraordinary composition around the Lord's Prayer: both may have been thinking in terms of 'the glory of God and the recreation of the spirit'.

Early Organ Chorales

It is uncertain what precisely many, even most, of Bach's chorale preludes were written for. Are they preludes? Many seem to be harmonised tunes with little interludes between the lines of each verse of text. Did the more unified pieces serve as prelude to the hymn sung by the congregation? Or did they alternate with the congregation in the centuries-old tradition of *alternatim* music, familiar to both Protestant and Roman Catholic organists? Scheidt, writing a century before Bach was at Weimar, did not know chorale preludes as such; his pieces were interludes played either between verses of the hymn (which themselves may have been unaccompanied) or in place of them (some settings have the same number of variations as the hymn had verses). For him, the organ did not even accompany the congregation; his interlude over, the organist sat silent while the congregation sang their verse. Variations or partitas on hymn-tunes have a further purpose. Bach, Böhm, Buxtehude, and so on back to Scheidt, were writing variations of a kind developed about 1600 by Sweelinck, organist of the Oude Kerk, Amsterdam, where not only were hymns unaccompanied but the organ remained silent throughout the Service. Such sets of variations were strictly recital pieces, played in the organ concerts held daily in the largest churches of Amsterdam, Haarlem and elsewhere.

Variations on any kind of tune, sacred or secular, are also obviously suitable for domestic music-making. Thus while one can be reasonably sure that this piece (which dates from the Weimar years) was indeed a congregational hymn with little interludes played by the organist between the *lines* of the hymn:

Ex. 2
BWV 729

it could well be that the next piece has another purpose. A movement from the partita BWV 766, the texture suggests performance
on the harpsichord, perhaps the Italianate instrument of two 8'
stops then familiar throughout Germany:

Ex. 3
BWV 766 (Partita VI)

This is not to raise useless questions about organ versus harpsichord
– although it is true that the harpsichord will play better the
'clumsy' keyboard-spacing which every commentator on Bach has
felt free to criticise in these partitas – but to point out the many
possible functions of works based on hymn-tunes. Supposing
these partitas indeed to be J. S. Bach's, they must be early works,
possibly written before Bach held a church post. Forkel claims
that he began to compose *Partite diverse* 'already when he was at
Arnstadt'. Although there is no particular plan in the organisation
of the variations, each movement does follow a regular, formalised
type. Inventiveness shows itself in the new way of treating old
patterns, rather than in creating new patterns. Some of the
variations, especially those with either optional or obbligato pedal,
resemble the 'closed form' chorale preludes familiar in the

Orgelbüchlein, i.e. short one-verse organ-harmonisations without interludes breaking the melody in the top part.

Although it may be difficult to accept the interlude convention of Ex. 2, it must be pointed out that it was known in other parts of Protestant Europe, including England. Judging by the story told by Charles Burney about the Cathedral music in Bremen, the interludes played by German organists between the lines were often as bad as those in London; the runs in Bach's 'In dulci jubilo' (Ex. 2) were at least full of Christmas exuberance and therefore relevant in a general way. Musical relevance must be the aim also of organ chorales played between verses of a hymn or after it, or indeed at any other point in the Service. Moreover, a chorale melody rarely had the simple associations known today outside Germany; it was often sung to two or more different texts (as 'O Mensch bewein' was to the Whitsuntide text 'Jauchz, Erd und Himmel') and obviously its organ-setting must show which text was concerned. Although the tune widely known as 'O Haupt voll Blut und Wunden' ('O sacred head sore wounded') is familiar also in a quite different version in the *Christmas Oratorio*, how many organists now think of yet a third version: its original text as a love-song in Hans Leo Hassler's *Lustgarten neuer teutscher Gesäng* (1601)? On the other hand, many organ chorales have only an approximate relevance to the meaning of the text, even when that text is concerned with some of the most solemn matters. Among those accepted as early works, 'Christ lag in Todesbanden' (BWV 718) is a chorale fantasia employing musical devices that can be seen as abstract musical ideas rather than word-paintings. An opening melody-with-running-bass similar to the first variation in Böhm's partitas is followed by a jig section in Buxtehude's manner; this in turn is followed by a section based on echo figures formulated by Tunder and others, and the work ends with a toccata section of general German type. The whole makes 77 bars, the last, by the way, varying from source to source. It may not be beyond commentators to trace these 77 bars in certain ideas suggested by the text; but it is hard to see them as 'expressive' of anything, or even so potentially expressive as the variations on the same chorale in Cantata 4.

The straightforward duties of the organist at Arnstadt and Mühlhausen may have allowed the composer to develop techniques learnt in Ohrdruf and Lüneburg, but there are too many uncertainties about the dating and even the authenticity of 'early works' – which sometimes means merely 'incompetent works' – to be able to follow out this idea. It is possible, for example, that not one of the 'youthful' preludes BWV 741–765 is by J. S. Bach; sources give no proof of their authenticity, and for such a prelude as BWV 749 ('Herr Jesu Christ, dich zu uns wend' ') it is impossible to say if the work is by Johann Christoph Bach imitating his teacher Pachelbel, or the young J. S. Bach imitating his elder brother, or any reasonably proficient composer of the so-called 'central German areas'. On the other hand, better preludes exist to suggest J. S. Bach intelligently following his models and writing good, individual pieces. The musical style of 'Vom Himmel hoch' (BWV 700) resembles that of Pachelbel in its particular fugato treatment of chorale lines with a cantus firmus (i.e. the theme in long notes) on the pedal; 'Nun freut euch' (BWV 734) already shows both a sense of phrase-structure and great confidence in cantus firmus techniques. As a piece originally written on two staves, 'Nun freut euch' shows how such a theme can be played either by pedal or by what Brahms is said to have called 'the tenor thumb'.

Early Preludes and Fugues

In the case of the early preludes and fugues, it has been suggested that a work can be placed in the composer's development by its degree of coherent organisation. Certainly a line of development – not necessarily of progress – can be assumed to exist between, say, the D minor Toccata and Fugue (BWV 565)[1] and the B minor (BWV 544). But how early is the first, how late the second? Were they written for similar purposes? Although organists no doubt found opportunities for playing preludes and fugues in the Service it is by no means clear at what point in the liturgy they played them. Do the flashy, toccata-like passages in many of the earlier preludes suggest that they were heard at the end of the Service? The 'preluding' or *fantasieren* heard then and referred to in eighteenth-century sources suggests extemporisation. There are also hints enough that any public or private trials of skill between organists would concern preludes and fugues as well as extempore

[1] The distinction between 'toccata', 'prelude' and 'fantasia' is doubtful since it is not certain what the composer originally called them, if anything at all.

variations. The fugue technique was, after all, traditional. Many chorale 'preludes' took fugal or near-fugal form; conventions were strong, and many of J. S. Bach's techniques and even specific details of figuration, motifs, sequences, etc., were common property. But the fugal movement of a 'prelude and fugue' is altogether a bigger conception; its shape is as characteristic as its contrapuntal technique.

Although the main sections toccata–fugue–toccata of the D minor Toccata and Fugue (BWV 565) are said to be 'northern' in style, they show an undeniably masterful personality quite unlike anything to be found in the work of the Hanseatic organists. The form may be conventional but the details are not. Specific devices, like the repeated notes on the same A as a violin open string, may remind us of the Italian string music with which the composer was becoming increasingly familiar. No autograph copy of BWV 565 is known, and nobody is ever likely to discover whether it was written before, during or after the visit to Lübeck to hear Buxtehude in the winter of 1705–6. Nobody knows if this is the original version of the work, or even if D minor was the original key, though this is likely. The G minor Prelude and Fugue (BWV 535) is almost certainly of the Weimar period, yet there is a version of it known to have been written in about 1705. Other works are also known in several versions: there is an earlier and a later version of the A major Prelude and Fugue (BWV 536), and while the C minor Prelude and Fugue (BWV 549) is no doubt an early work a version in D minor is also known, written or copied at much the same time. Both Preludes and Fugues, BWV 536 and 549, may show attempts at musical 'unity'; BWV 535 hints in the prelude at the fugue subject, though this is probably accidental and in any case is not exploited further. That the fugue subject of BWV 549 resembles certain motifs in the prelude is more plausible, especially since the fugue leads naturally into the closing toccata section.

There are, then, interesting points to be observed about many of these pieces, for instance their overall organisation The sectional nature of such works as the Prelude and Fugue in A minor (BWV 551) is of a certain kind: as in toccatas of both the southern and northern composers, section seems to grow out of section, some fugal some not, but all fitting together in a common pulse or beat, a common level of intensity and perhaps even a common tempo. There are references here to a kind of counterpoint written by such distant composers as Sweelinck, just as there are characteristics in both the pedal prelude and fugue subject of BWV 531 (C major) that remind the player of Reinken or Böhm. Several of the earlier fugues such as BWV 531 (C major), 532 (D major) and 533 (E minor) have a characteristic tendency towards block chords, especially as a means of throwing the theme into relief, and it is a style that could come from almost anywhere:

Ex. 4
BWV 533 (bar 19)

Such a device is quite different from the relatively homophonic passages found in later works, where homophony often results from a surfeit of polyphony; it also has the effect of bridging the stylistic gap between prelude and fugue. Deliberate disunity between sections, however, is not necessarily a fault; the E major Toccata and Fugue (BWV 566) has four long major sections, each with its own form and each (except for the penultimate section) closing on a perfect cadence. Although the subject of the second fugue is related to the first – its shortened triple-time version and its repeated notes are reminiscent of Frescobaldi's *canzone* subjects – it is tempting to see the hand of the master in the way that a motif, promising (like the subject itself) to become a tiresomely predictable sequence, is lifted out towards the fine cadence:

Ex. 5
BWV 566 (bar 28)

Ped.

It is therefore disconcerting to find that the ascription to Bach is unreliable and that he may have had nothing to do with the piece.

The element of display, of organist's showmanship, that expresses itself in, for example, pedal passages of neither immense difficulty nor harmonic subtlety, such as the G major (BWV 550) or the C minor (BWV 549), or in triadic figures for the manuals in either prelude (A major, BWV 536) or fugue (G major, BWV 550), may be taken as a relatively immature characteristic. BWV 536, which exists in two versions, was probably revised at Weimar – the top e' required for pedals could have been found there, but, alas, compass is a poor indication of when, where and why a piece was written. BWV 550 also requires e', as the D minor Toccata (BWV 565) requires the almost equally rare bottom C sharp. There is no knowing why such pieces have the compass they do have (they might be transcriptions or revisions, or altered by the copyist, or written for a particular organ) and we must look into more essential matters before we can assume that the composer wrote a given work for the rather special conditions of Weimar.

Weimar

The Weimar appointment was the turning-point in the composer's life, and the effect on Bach of this particular move can be easily imagined. His new salary was nearly double that at Mühlhausen; there was a rise in social standing when an organist moved from the secondary church of a Free Imperial City to the chapel of a ducal court; there were new musical possibilities for an organist working in the court of a duke known to encourage music as a Lutheran means towards 'the greater glory of God'. There are interesting signs of change in the composer's musical development: he got to know important composers like Telemann and

J. G. Walther; he met with the immediately striking characteristics of the Italian concerto style – a widening of musical horizons that is reflected in the church cantatas of 1713–16; he began to travel not so much 'to hear as many good organists' and other musicians as possible (as the Obituary describes his earlier visits to Lübeck, Hamburg and Celle) but as a virtuoso player himself, writing music 'such as must make one esteem the man highly', as Mattheson wrote of him.[1]

More interesting still is that from at least 1703 Bach began to make his own collections of important music for organ and for other instruments, both his own and other composers'. With that taste for collecting and with a musical background based on elements fairly easy to trace, Bach has become the ideal subject for biographers anxious to show what led a man to be 'the culmination of an era'. But other composers did likewise. J. G. Walther, for instance, transcribed and arranged more Italian concertos than Bach is known to have done and indeed it is partly due to Walther's care and industry that we know as much as we do of Bach's works for organ.

Both the Obituary and other early sources point out that it was at Weimar that Bach 'wrote most of his organ works'. This is what would be expected, since at Köthen and Leipzig he was not the organist nor did he ever again have any liturgical reason for writing organ music once he had left Weimar. According to the Obituary, even at Weimar after 1714 his duties lay 'mainly in composing church pieces' or cantatas. The period 1708–17 found him not only a masterly performer and maturing composer, but one situated in circumstances very conducive to a developing organ-style. The Obituary says that he was invited to Weimar after he had visited the Residence and 'had the opportunity to be heard by the reigning duke'; it was 'the pleasure his Grace took in his playing' that 'fired him with the desire to try every possible artistry in his treatment of the organ'. Certainly the scope and variety of organ works from this period are immense and over-whelmingly rich – from the chorale preludes of the *Orgelbüchlein* to most of the major preludes and fugues, from little miscellaneous pieces to complete concerto transcriptions, from trio movements to the Passacaglia. It is a platitude to point out that each group

[1] *Das beschützte Orchester* (Hamburg, 1717), p. 222, the first known printed reference to J. S. Bach.

contains the best pieces of their type ever written; it is more fruitful to think of them amongst other works from this period – such cantatas as BWV 161, 'Komm, du süsse Todesstunde' (1715) with its confident and original sense of scoring, vocal writing, and even (though this is not very common) solo organ. Such music is not only that of a composer very alive to new sounds and to the potential of instruments at his disposal (including in this case the voice of a virtuoso countertenor) but suggests what such a composer could do in the realm of organ chorales. Indeed, its five parts are more intricate than those of any organ chorale of that period; they have already extended the frontiers of contrapuntal pieces based on chorales. In other words, many movements in the Weimar church cantatas have a close relevance to the composer's organ-music of that period, showing his sense of scoring and texture on one hand and his maturing attitude to chorales and hymn-melodies on the other. In some respects, notably texture, Ex. 6 is indeed more advanced than much of the contemporary organ-music of Bach, while in others, notably harmony, both have reached new standards.

Ex. 6

The picture, then, is of a large group of organ pieces in different forms and styles, written for different purposes, spread over nearly a decade and often containing only internal evidence as a guide to the position in the composer's output. As before, many of the preludes and fugues do not exist in copies made by the composer, while other pieces such as the Passacaglia and the trios are accepted only reluctantly as organ music by some people. In many respects chorale preludes offer fewer problems.

Italianate Works

By late 1716 Bach was writing ritornello movements of an Italian kind in church cantatas: an element known to Bach very likely from string concertos and not then common musical property. Many organ works are Italian in theme or form; but style is more elusive, and it is wrong to think of an 'Italian period' in the composer's work.

In the way it applies its theme to both duple and triple time, the Canzona in D minor (BWV 588) is reminiscent of Frescobaldi himself (of whose *Fiori musicali* of 1635 Bach signed a copy in 1714) as well as his German imitators, just as the *Alla breve* (BWV 589)[1] follows the general idiom of much Italian string and keyboard music. The contrapuntal suspensions of the *Alla breve* are remarkably like certain passages in Corelli's string sonatas and concertos, Op. I–VI. The phrase *alla breve* implies a style of counterpoint as

[1] See Ex. 20 (i) on p. 59.

much as a tempo, and such a style was to find itself often in Bach's maturest music. It is not known whether the Italian Pastorale (BWV 590) was following a model, or even if the movements as we know them belong together. The first three of the four movements resemble several Italian organ pastorals of the seventeenth century, not only in the drone and simple harmonies but in the melodic details. The two movements in binary form are more suite-like, and there is little exclusively Italian about such shapes. Similarly, one may doubt whether the implied binary form of the F minor Prelude (BWV 534) is an Italianate feature *per se*. And was there a conscious following of the Italian concerto idea when the composer gave the big C major Toccata (BWV 564) a slow movement with conventional basso continuo pedal part? Although Bach must have come into contact with at least some kinds of Italian music at Lüneburg, is Spitta right to see definite elements of Italian arias in those two-part chorale-variations of Böhm and Bach (e.g. 'Christ lag in Todesbanden', BWV 718) that have a bass theme running counter to the melody?

The concerto arrangements are the most obvious example of Italian idioms and forms impinging on Bach's music for organ. Like the organ version of the very Italianate violin fugue in G minor (the D minor fugue, BWV 539), there is doubt that the arrangements were made by Bach himself; likewise the fugues on a theme of Corelli (BWV 579) and supposedly Legrenzi (BWV 574). But the best concertos, in A minor and D minor, are conveniently accepted as authentic. They are concertos in the sense of the published *Italian Concerto* for harpsichord, i.e. works for one player making use of the contrasting manuals of one instrument. One must look elsewhere, for example Cantata BWV 29 (1731), to obtain some idea of what the composer would have done had he worked movements for organ and big orchestra into fully-fledged concertos. Such movements have little in common with the simple works of Vivaldi.

It is in the concerto-arrangements that two manuals are consistently registered, by Bach (D minor) or copyist (A minor). Both were originally concertos by Vivaldi for two violins and orchestra, and published as such, though Bach made use of manuscript versions. The distinction is between *Oberwerk* (Great Organ) and *Rückpositiv* (Chair Organ). As had long been customary in north and central Germany, the *Rückpositiv* is often given the solo part. But this manual is also expected to play accompaniments, probably on some sharp and glittering combination of stops:

Ex. 7
BWV 593 (bar 54)

The fine D minor concerto (BWV 596) did not appear in the original *Bachgesellschaft* edition because a note written by W. F. Bach on his father's copy (*c.* 1714–17) led the editors into believing it by Friedemann, as he claimed. The Concerto avoids the top manual d''' by putting Vivaldi's opening passage for two violins down an octave and registering it for 4′ stop(s). Organists ignoring this registration are totally changing the character of the section. The Weimar organ had no *Rückpositiv*, so who is responsible for labelling the various second-manual passages thus? In BWV 596 first-movement sections for second manual are labelled *Brustwerk* not *Rückpositiv*, which accords with the Weimar organ's specification. It is also significant that the fugue movement appears to be played without change of manual, Bach omitting Vivaldi's specified echo effects: this seems to be evidence that German organists understood fugues as one-manual works, as did their French, Austrian and Italian colleagues. The first movement of BWV 596 also suggests that there was an assistant standing by to push in or pull out the stops; this may also be the implication of the sign *organo pleno* in BWV 593.[1] Such changes of tone are too

[1] If, as is likely, the manual coupler at Weimar came into play only when one of the keyboards was pushed or pulled, coupling would have been

quick for the organist himself. Changes of manual are easier to make, and it is significant that the concerto movement of this group which has more manual changes specified than any authenticated piece by Bach – the first movement of the C major Concerto (BWV 595) – is longer by nearly a quarter than the same movement arranged for harpsichord without manual changes (BWV 984). These six concertos (BWV 592–7) are in no sense a group of pieces and the authenticity of at least one of them (BWV 597) is uncertain. Nevertheless, although four of them also contain movements of doubtful effectiveness, they do represent an important body of music well known by a highly receptive composer, and often hint at themes, textures and organ-styles met with in other, more central, organ-works of the Weimar period.

Weimar Organ Chorales

Much has been made of the note written by J. G. Ziegler in 1746 that when 'playing chorales, I was taught by my instructor Capellmeister Bach . . . to play them not indifferently but according to the *Affect* of the words'. Although it is not at all clear whether this refers to hymns or to organ chorales, the remark seems to give a clue to the beauty and 'affecting' quality of so many of the Weimar preludes. It was at Weimar, according to one modern writer, that the composer 'attempted to express subjectively the message of the hymn', a popular view that can at times disguise his indebtedness, even in the *Orgelbüchlein*, to keyboard idioms and formulae known in secular music of the previous century. In the later collections of organ chorales (*Clavierübung III*, Schübler, the so-called Eighteen) the composer begins by taking over historic prelude-types, continuing in new styles, becoming progressively more melodic and even at times doing without contrapuntal imitation. It is interesting that the Obituary reports on Bach's extemporised chorale variations at Hamburg in 1720 not in terms of the 'affecting', subjective nature of his interpretation but in terms of its objective variety and length – qualities most likely to strike one organist as impressive in the work of another, or most likely to remain in the memory of the performer himself. Bach 'performed extempore the chorale "An

impossible in the course of a piece. *Organo pleno* must therefore indicate an increase in the number of stops.

Wasserflüssen Babylon" at great length (for almost half an hour) and in different ways, just as the better organists of Hamburg in the past had been used to do at the Saturday vespers', i.e. at the extra-liturgical Services that often grew into concerts. The authors of the Obituary had probably had this report years before from the composer himself.

It is the variety of the Weimar and Leipzig works that arouses admiration, not only in the number of ways a technique is applied but in the variety of result achieved by one and the same technique for different melodies. One can only guess that the naive, diminished seventh chromaticism of 'Allein Gott in der Höh'' (BWV 715) typifies the Arnstadt years – perhaps the 'many strange tones' the organist was rebuked for introducing into the hymns – and that it gradually gave way to a maturer sense of harmony. The 'motet' type of organ chorale, one in which each line is the basis of a contrapuntal paragraph in the plain, old-fashioned Scheidt manner, becomes fluent and stylish. Although void of harmonic surprise, the smooth successful linearity of this style should not be underestimated (see Example 19(ii)). Nor should the brilliant use of organ be thought of as alien to a spirit attempting 'to express subjectively the message of a hymn'. The five-part prelude on 'Wir glauben all' (BWV 740) may be hard to see as a bold, virile affirmation of Faith, and seems rather a contemplative exercise alike for performer (double pedal, high left hand) and composer (imitative and ornamented cantus firmus). But both performer's and composer's skills in 'Valet will ich dir geben', BWV 736, are called for to achieve 'the message of the hymn':

Ex. 8
BWV 736

The pedal part is a splendid example of the cantus firmus technique, where the theme in long notes is left to penetrate the harmonies above. As Arnold Schlick appreciated two centuries before, it is a technique excellently suited to the organ, but it was left to Bach to develop a version which subtly and implicitly incorporates the same theme in the upper parts at the same time.

Orgelbüchlein

The Hamburg recital of 1720 found the composer playing something in the nature of an 'objective' partita and it may be significant that the chorale concerned ('By the waters of Babylon') is not one associated intimately with the Christian mysteries: it was one of the non-seasonal chorales listed but never set in the unfinished *Orgelbüchlein*.

The *Orgelbüchlein* is to all organists a work of unique beauty, often allowed to eclipse other Weimar works, including those later collected and revised as the Eighteen. The *Büchlein* or album was planned to contain preludes on 164 chorales; but only 45 were set, and blank, titled pages were left for the others. Since one of the 45 ('Liebster Jesu') was set twice and others were marked *alio modo* (theme set 'in another fashion'), it seems that at least some were intended to have more than one version. While many of those set suggest that the composer found in them particular qualities inspiring organ preludes, no one knows the reasons for his choice of chorales. Beginning naturally with Advent, the unfinished contents may reflect only the workings of his well-ordered mind, and examination of all 164 themes and texts does not allow one to agree with Schweitzer that he picked out only 'those of which the strong pictorial or characteristic quality seemed to make . . . especially suitable for music' while others 'could only be developed as pure music, not in their poetic or pictorial aspects'.

The *Orgelbüchlein* was probably begun in 1714 or even earlier, nine of the pieces completed before the end of 1714; work seems to have stopped in 1715 or 1716, and the title-page was written only towards the end of the Köthen period much later. It is uncertain when the scheme of the collection was drawn up; the old idea that it was planned and a fair copy made while the composer was under arrest for four weeks in November 1717 is unfounded. At Leipzig in or after about 1740, BWV 620 was revised and a copy made by Kirnberger or some other copyist, BWV 613 was added to fill in a gap in the Christmas cycle, and the 1½-bar fragment 'O Traurigkeit' was added to the Passion cycle. Occasionally an *Orgelbüchlein* prelude may apply a technique reminiscent of vocal music of the time, such as the ostinato technique known also in the earlier cantatas. Those that are shown by small details of handwriting to be the earliest sometimes include idiomatic keyboard motifs typical of the earlier preludes and fugues, such as the device of turning what is basically one line into two contrapuntal, antiphonal parts (left hand of 'Der Tag, der ist so freudenreich', BWV 605). The order follows to some extent that of the chorales in the Weimar hymn-books of 1708 and 1713, three chorales found only in the latter (including 'In dir ist Freude'). The Weimar organ, rebuilt in 1711–13, would have had its varieties well demonstrated by the four Advent preludes (BWV 599–602), as no doubt the same organ, had it been rebuilt in 1714, would have been by 'In dir ist Freude' (BWV 615). Italian influences are not at all obvious, though the predominantly triadic, non-modulating style of some of them has been taken as an Italian feature, and consequently the canonic treatment of BWV 619 is regarded as less mature than that of BWV 620.

The *Orgelbüchlein*, then, is a collection of organ pieces based on chorales which follow the church year from Advent onwards, apparently one for each day concerned; of the forty listed for the period from Advent to Easter thirty-two were composed. The final twelve do not belong to seasons but relate to other functions or aspects of church or private worship. Formally each 'prelude' resembles a one-verse variation from a partita, but in concentration of style, uniformity and command of motivic development, exposition of text and (at their best) complete mastery of organ texture, the collection was something quite new. The particular technique of 'melody chorale' is found only rarely elsewhere, and in some ways the preludes are little more than playings through of the hymn-tune. Considering the importance of the melodies, it is interesting that by no means all are directed to be played on a solo manual; some of those specifying two manuals (such as 'Christe, du Lamm Gottes', BWV 619) do so to give two canonic or imitative parts to each hand, and not to bring out the melody. The composer's own description on the title-page was 'Organ Album, in which instruction is given a beginner at the organ in working out a chorale in many different ways, also in perfecting himself in playing pedals, the pedals being treated in these chorales as wholly obbligato'. While no one would expect the title-page to say 'in which instruction is given in writing succinct, beautiful and perfect preludes', much less 'in which instruction is given in expressing texts graphically and symbolically', it is important to note that Bach specifies three aims: (i) instructing the beginner; (ii) instructing him how to write in many varied musical styles and techniques; and (iii) practice-music for pedal-playing. Pieces written as harmonisations of chorales at Weimar nearly ten years earlier thus received at Köthen a title-page which – like the newly composed *Inventions* – expressed a new aim. They are now 'instruction for beginners', useful to a busy teacher who was probably not going to play them again himself during a Service.

Each approach to Bach's organ chorales – their beauty, their 'symbolism', their mastery – is rewarding. Much has been made of the pictorialism, and while some interpretations are doubtful to say the least, others are not. I do not see the inner parts of 'Der Tag, der ist so freudenreich' as picturing the rocking cradle of the nativity, nor the lively pedal to 'Alle Menschen müssen sterben', as picturing the vision of eternal life described in the hymn-text. But nobody could doubt the falling sevenths of 'Durch Adams Fall' or the rising motifs of the resurrection chorale, 'Erstanden ist der Heil'ge Christ'. Rising and falling lines are straightforward musical devices, literally not symbolically pictorial. But do the runs of 'Vom Himmel kam der Engel Schar' describe the rushing angels of the nativity? Does the dragging motif of 'Mit Fried' und Freud' suggest the dragging feet of the venerable author of the 'Nunc dimittis'? Perhaps. Many players may be puzzled by one commentator finding ten appearances of a countersubject in 'Dies sind die heil'gen zehn Gebot' (The Ten Commandments); even more may wonder at the significance of the supposed fact. It is doubtful if any listener need feel obliged to see the canonic or *imitative* treatment of 'Hilf Gott' as expressing the *imitation* of Christ in the text: is it even certain that Bach used the word *imitatio* in both senses? More relevant is the unquestionable reference many passages make to the hymn-text bar by bar.[1] The best-known example of this is the phrase in BWV 622 that corresponds to the words 'enduring the cross' in the original hymn:

Ex. 9
BWV 622
(i) Chorale

wohl

(ii)

an   dem   Kreu _ ze   lan _ _ ge.

adagissimo

It is puzzling to find this exquisite chord of C flat described by one scholar as merely an example of the flattened third (G flat in the key of E flat major) found also in Froberger, Buxtehude and

Böhm. It is more likely a highly original form of quasi-'Neapolitan' chord, the more effective here for appearing at the end of a long prelude.

Two other fruitful approaches to the *Orgelbüchlein* concern technical devices. One of the most remarkable features of most of the settings is that the accompaniment and the motifs of which it is composed are newly invented and are not related thematically to the melody. This in itself distinguishes them from so many fugal chorales of earlier and contemporary composers, including Bach himself in other pieces. The ostinato motif in 'In dir ist Freude' is an extreme example: it has nothing to do with the melody except that it is its countersubject for this piece. Usually a three-part accompaniment runs or plods or sings gently below the melody, and even if it looks like becoming imitative of the melody, it tends to go its own way:

Ex. 10
BWV 613

Other accompaniments are more vertical, less horizontal. The variety is immense, and while certain devices like the throbbing bass of 'Ich ruf' zu dir' may remind the player of similar things elsewhere (such as 'O Schmerz' in the *St Matthew Passion*) these similarities should not be overestimated. Other characteristics may enable us to trace the composer's developing technique: the earlier preludes tend to have the bass part end with the melody, while the inner parts continue until impetus fades at the end (e.g.

'Vom Himmel hoch'). Later preludes have a pedal more independent of the chorale-melody's cadence (e.g. 'Christum wir
sollen loben schon'). As well as such variety of technique, claimed
on the title-page, also striking is the harmonic language at certain
points, especially in some of the nine canonic preludes. The
dissonances arise in 'Liebster Jesu' from the motion – especially
the accented passing-notes – of the accompaniment, rather than
from the canonic voices themselves; while particularly impressive
is the masterful understanding of diatonic harmony that enables the
composer in 'Gottes Sohn ist kommen' to skirt the abyss of
harmonic implausibility and pull the composition through to fluent
concordance:

Ex. 11
BWV 600 (bar 6)

Weimar and Later Preludes and Fugues

Forkel's first category of Bach's organ works is 'Grand Preludes
and Fugues, with obbligato pedal. Their number cannot be
precisely ascertained; but I believe it does not exceed a dozen.
At least, with all my inquiries for many years, at the best sources,
I have not been able to collect more than 12'. Various reasons may
account for Forkel's failure to find more than twelve (BWV 533,
535, 538, 539, 540, 541, 543, 544, 545a, 546, 547, 548 plus the
printed 'St Anne'); it must be open to doubt how useful they were
to organists, how many players would have had the ability or
desire – and how many churches would have provided the

opportunity – to perform them. Plenty of later eighteenth-century organ-music is difficult to play, but Pastor Bellermann's report of Bach in 1743 describes the demands of these preludes and fugues admirably: 'by using his feet alone (his hands doing nothing or doing something quite different) he can bring out such a wonderful, lively and rapid concord of sound on the organ that others are scarcely able to do likewise with their hands.' What precisely it was that in 1717 led Mattheson, a musician used to a quite different musical climate, to 'esteem highly the man' is unknown, but any of the great preludes and fugues would strike a contemporary as remarkable. Most resemble little else of their period in technical demand, overall conception and details of style.

Nobody is ever likely to know which of Bach's preludes and fugues can be ascribed to the early Weimar years and which to the Arnstadt-Mühlhausen period. It has already been noted that the Prelude and Fugue in A major (BWV 536) was probably revised at Weimar, but an earlier version exists in the composer's hand. It is interesting that the smooth effortless counterpoint of its 3/4 fugue treats the subject almost as an ostinato. The Jig Fugue (BWV 577) – which may not be the work of Bach and, like BWV 532, resembles fugues by both Pachelbel and Buxtehude – is quite different; it contains longer episodes, and its sequences (derived from the subject) lead one to see strong Italian influences. Some other works probably of the late Arnstadt period (D major, BWV 532) or early Weimar period (G major, BWV 550) are showy pieces, with a narrow harmonic spectrum and conventional, sequential suspensions. They imply a certain keyboard panache in the writing of both prelude and fugue. The tendency towards square phrases, characteristic of other composers of the period, is often counteracted by other features: for example, in the G major prelude there is a calculated ambiguity over the pulse. Is it 3/2 or 2/2?

Mild harmonies, conventional sequences, alla breve suspensions and keyboard showiness are also to be found in the Fantasia in G (BWV 572). Its obvious indebtedness to other styles has sent devotees looking for parallels in the organ music of north and south Germany, France and even Italy. The nearest parallel to the sustained section is the French *plein jeu* interlude. More directly Italianate is the *adagio* movement of the C major Toccata, Adagio and Fugue (BWV 564). Its four sections do not follow the same plan as those of the Buxtehudian Prelude and Fugue in D (BWV 532), any more than Buxtehude's own preludes-and-fugues share a common plan. Very short phrases are typical of the whole of BWV 564: the rests, gaps and occasional repeated notes in all three movements contrast with the sustained, chromatic flow of the 10-bar *grave* section, a passage easily outstripping Buxtehude's and Böhm's attempts at the same thing. For once the short phrases of the toccata make the use of two manuals plausible, though still not necessary. A passage like the following belongs ultimately to the Buxtehude style, but its idiom is nevertheless highly original and certainly not like other three-part music of the period:

Ex. 12

BWV 564 (bar 67)

The frequent charm of such pieces should not be forgotten; the melodic extension in bars 3–4 of the motif in bar 1 is a good example, as is the refusal of the fugue to end boisterously or rhetorically. It ends low down, pedal-less and staccato; nobody should feel justified in tampering with it.

How many of the other preludes and fugues in one version or another (not necessarily the original) were separated by a slow movement is unknown. The big C major (BWV 545/545a) may have had a middle movement in the form of a trio, and an eighteenth-century version in B flat contains three movements. The G major (BWV 541) was copied by another organist (J. P. Kellner) with the first thirteen bars of the E minor *un poco allegro* from the Fourth Organ Sonata placed between prelude and fugue. Bach's own copy of 1740 or later may be based on a version from *c.* 1712. Repeated notes are still characteristic of what seems to be a maturing Weimar style – not only the repeated notes of the fugue theme (an element less exclusively north German than usually thought) but the rhythmic, often homophonic repetition of notes or chords. Although not particularly characteristic of either harpsichord music or of Italian concertos, repeated notes and chords give BWV 541 a texture quite different from the most mature works. They, too, often repeat notes or chords, but to different effect:

Ex. 13

(i) BWV 541 (bar 61)

(ii) BWV 544 (bar 81)

The repeated notes in the second example are there to create lush suspensions rather than clear, spiky rhythms. The beautifully rich writing of this B minor prelude (BWV 544) is geared towards an almost heavy sensuality, one very much endangered today by organists clipping the pedal rhythm, i.e. taking the semiquaver too short. It should sound heavy and deliberate.

Vague and personal though some interpretations of Bach are, there is certainly some justification for seeing the best of the Weimar works as conscious attempts at rhythmic and harmonic excitement. A work like the first movement of the Toccata and Fugue in F (BWV 540, 1713?) must first of all have been written either for a special organ (the top pedal f′ could have been found at Weissenfels and in one of the Köthen churches) or at least – since there is no copy in Bach's hand to give incontrovertible proof that the f′ belonged to an original version[1] – it was written for a special player, himself or a pupil perhaps. The rhythmic excitement of the toccata is based on the somewhat Italianate figure ♪♫ ; the harmonic devices are also dramatic and rhetorical, rather than subtle. While the Neapolitan sixths may slip by unnoticed, the unique interrupted cadences do not, nor can anybody fail to be stirred by the ensuing sequences. The sense of sustained climax in the second part of the toccata, caused by the busy figuration after a big perfect cadence, is most unusual.

The skill shown in the F minor Prelude and Fugue (BWV 534), known only from a late copy, is of a less obvious kind, but is none the less unusual. The prelude aims at unity of texture and theme by means of little obsessive figures and rhythms, the whole blending into one remarkably unified piece; the fugue on the other hand aims at varying texture and, like the prelude, invents interesting sequences and exploits sequential devices throughout. Both BWV 534 and 540 could be seen as examples of a mastery perhaps recently acquired, a mastery concerned in different ways with extending motifs and melodic/harmonic ideas – with 'development' in its musical sense. The motifs – little groups of four or more notes – are not yet particularly original, but their concentrated working-out is very distinguished.

[1] The pedal goes above e′ only once, in bar 156. Bars 151–66 may have originated as a skilful composer's addition to a pedal cadenza already perfectly adequate.

The fugue and prelude of the Toccata in F (BWV 540) are each found alone and unpaired in various eighteenth-century collections of organ music, and the contrast between the two movements is certainly severe. Much the same can be said of several others, including the Dorian Toccata and Fugue (BWV 538) and the C minor Prelude and Fugue (BWV 546). Some have considered the prelude and fugue of BWV 546 to have been composed at widely differing periods. The C minor Fantasia (BWV 562) is indeed known as a separate piece, but it seems to have been followed by one fugue in an early version and by another (in 6/4, incomplete but extant in autograph manuscript) in a version made perhaps as late as the final Leipzig years. In at least two ways, the Fantasia is most interesting: its contrapuntal organisation, fluent and original, and its appoggiatura-full harmonies. The appoggiaturas are not unimportant grace-notes or a mere notational quirk. The piece could hardly be taken as a model for extemporised ornaments as there are few if any comparable passages elsewhere, but there is something crucial here to an understanding of Bach's changing harmonic style. This is to be seen especially in the rising appoggiaturas of this piece. The taste hints at *le goût français*, of course, and it is not difficult to find similar but smaller-scaled pieces by de Grigny and others.

More straightforward formally is another contrapuntal prelude in C minor, the first movement of Prelude and Fugue BWV 537. Like BWV 562 and perhaps the F minor prelude (BWV 534), it is a binary movement without the repeat-marks and double-barlines. Unlike BWV 562, it ends on an imperfect cadence and so leads to the fugue: the prelude proper ends in the penultimate bar and is followed by the descending bass of the conventional Phrygian cadence of the period – something unusual in organ music. The fugue is an ABA da capo movement, the third section a repeat (more fully harmonised) of the opening, the middle section a further double fugue built partly on a theme running out of the original countersubject. Although this makes it appear a formal *tour de force*, in fact it is a very direct piece, full of the most marvellous organ counterpoint and beauty of line. The fugue is not particularly long: it is as if the ABA form frankly acknowledges that the opening exposition has already provided passages that could not be bettered:

Ex. 14
BWV 537 (bar 18)

and that therefore there must be something new in the middle. The principle is quite different from the fugue of the F major Toccata, where the texture is more traditional.

The C minor fugue ends on a multiple appoggiatura – not a remarkable device to generations nurtured on the Viennese classics, but one hinting at the composer's maturing harmonic language. In comparison, the Dorian Toccata and Fugue (BWV 538) – so called from the old-fashioned but insignificant omission of the flat key-signature – seems to be an earlier work, with its repeated chords and square rhythms. This is misleading, however, and one wonders how old the piece was when (according to a note on one early copy) it was played at the public opening of the Kassel organ in 1732. In some ways the work seems a deliberate tribute to the northern organ-schools, in its kind of manual work, its staccato chords, its pair of manuals required for the prelude (the copyist's terms are *Oberw* and *Pos* which may not refer to specific manuals), and the way they are used chiefly for chorus-contrasts rather than for trio-playing. On the other hand, the fugue subject is a typical product of a composer under southerly influences; its real virtue, one that has often resulted in its being underrated by non-composers, is that it allows the most marvellous counterpoints, stylish themes expanded at great length, often in stretto, always very well timed. Notice, for instance, that from the harmonic point of view the final pedal entry could appear a bar earlier than it does; it is delayed partly to let the preceding quavers lose impetus and achieve their own cadence, partly for a stretto.

The A minor (BWV 543) has a much simpler prelude, showing all the characteristics expected of the earlier Weimar years; like other works, it was revised later. The fugue resembles the harpsichord fugue made famous by Liszt (BWV 944) and has, so far as contrapuntal potential is concerned, a simple texture. Its fine theme may appear to some too fine for fugal development, and quite necessary is the toccata flourish at the end. A final entry on classical lines (as in BWV 538) would not convey the correct sense of climax.

The A minor Prelude and Fugue is relevant at this point because it serves as an example of a piece revised or found in other versions, if that is what BWV 944 is. As the very terms 'toccata', 'fantasia', 'prelude' are often unreliable, so constantly the possibility of other versions should be considered. An unusual instance is the C major Prelude and Fugue (BWV 545) where an 'old version' of the prelude begins in bar 4 of the familiar version. Probably at some point in the Leipzig period, the composer added a few bars to the beginning and end of a piece that, judging by the opening prelude of Book II of the *Forty-Eight*, seems to have been for Bach a kind of 'standard C major prelude'. Like the C minor (BWV 537), the fugue is notable for well-structured idiomatic sequences, not to mention one of organ literature's most effective final pedal entries. In both prelude and fugue the writing for manuals is expansive and the hands often find themselves moving in large leaps; this is true also of the pedals in the prelude, while in the fugue the theme results in a smoother pedal part. Once again, prelude and fugue seem complementary in their demands.

The other great C major Prelude and Fugue (BWV 547) is known from copies of the Leipzig period, but may well be regarded as a late Weimar piece. Harmonic surprises – i.e. distancing from the tonic – are still contrived not in terms of intricate progressions but simple dominant and diminished sevenths, as indeed is often the case in some of Bach's last compositions. Some of the most conspicuous characteristics are the 9/8 rhythm (which miraculously avoids the mundane and is no more to be performed as a jolly dance than the cantata movements it resembles), the pedal *quasi ostinato*, the particular manual figurations anticipating textures in the *Goldberg Variations*, the square Pachelbel-like fugue theme, and the delayed pedal entry. Unlike the delayed pedal entry in the little C minor (or D minor) fugue (BWV 549), the theme here is augmented and placed in stretto with the straight and inverted versions at the same time, in this combination anticipating the *Canonic Variations*, also in C major.

If such a survey has reinforced one's impression of the staggering variety and invention of these works, how even more striking is the G minor Fantasia and Fugue (BWV 542), for here is a prelude unlike anything else even in Bach's output. A story that gradually evolved was of the composer playing the work before Reinken in the Hamburg Katharinenkirche on his visit of 1720, basing the fugue theme on a 'Dutch folk-song' as a tribute to Reinken's origin and to one of his own fugues. Mattheson knew the fugue theme by 1725 and the movement is known from many copies. In fact, however, the theme has many possible originals, not least in the fertile brain of a prolific composer. That side of the Hamburg story cannot be sustained. Nor, so far as manual-compass is a guide, can the Fantasia have been played at the Katharinenkirche, though researches on the Jakobikirche organ, where Bach evidently hoped to succeed as organist, might establish a suitable compass there (the comparable Schnitger organ at the Nikolai-kirche, Hamburg, did have full compass). In short, the whole biographical issue is confusing and may for the moment be forgotten. Much more remarkable is the nature of the Fantasia, the fact that in most sources the fugue appears alone, the complete discrepancy between the fugue (in itself similar to middle-period Weimar fugues) and the Fantasia in harmonic language, melodic fluency and degree of intensity. The originality of the Fantasia lies partly in its figurations, harmonic suspensions and sequential modulations, partly in its tendency to burst into passionate runs (which encourages too many organists to change stops and manuals), and partly in its awareness of the ambivalence of the diminished seventh – an effect not far removed from certain cantata recitatives of Alessandro Scarlatti. Such sevenths can modulate in various directions and thereby achieve unexpected and novel progressions:

Ex. 15

(i) BWV 542 (bar 13)

(ii) (bar 20)

Other examples can be found there. Equally remarkable is the way passages of beguiling simplicity follow and intersperse these harmonic labyrinths.

The Passacaglia

Although the Passacaglia in C minor (BWV 582) is a kind of long prelude and fugue, the work deserves special attention because of its '21 variations, intertwined so ingeniously that one can never cease to be amazed' (in the words of Schumann). It thus stands somewhat apart from the rest of Bach's organ music. There is even plausible doubt as to its suitability for organ; at least, there has been a tradition in some quarters that (in the words of Forkel) the Passacaglia 'is rather for two claviers and pedal than for the organ' – i.e. for pedal-harpsichord. If Forkel saw a copy marked 'à 2 claviers et péd.', which is possible, he would simply have mis-understood the term *clavier* (manual) – provided that this is what his oddly written sentence means. Since the church Service gave no opportunity for such a piece – the name of which in any case must have suggested a secular dance to writers in the late eighteenth century – it is also reasonable to think of it as a chamber work. There is, in short, no sure answer, and the fact that the piece was written into the *Andreas Bach Buch*, a collection of miscellaneous keyboard music by various composers made by 1717 or 1719, does not carry the argument on one side or the other.

The work has several possible functions, one of which is that of a chamber study-piece; yet it is interesting that the first half of the passacaglia theme (the part of it that Bach uses for the following fugue) occurs in a church organ piece by André Raison. Raison was perhaps one of the 'old French composers' that Carl Philipp told Forkel his father admired. Unusually for Service music published by French composers, Raison's piece is also a passacaglia, though short and developed only as far as was required of Mass interludes. Bach's passacaglia naturally resembles ostinato works of Buxtehude but is unlike the chaconne types familiar in south Germany, except that Bach bases variations on one particular figure, in the established manner of Pachelbel, Kerl and others. The resemblance to Buxtehude lies in certain figurations, the developed organ-texture, and other more subjective aspects, such as the strange melancholy of the theme itself.

The plan of a 'Passacaglia and Fugue' is highly original and unusual. It is important, for instance, that Buxtehude's ostinato sections often come at the end of a fugue rather than before it. The whole origin and conception of the piece are puzzling, not least because the fugue has more than a few figurations in common with the G major Fugue (BWV 541) dated *c.* 1712. But that could perhaps be expected. Very intricate organisation has been seen to be behind this work, and its twenty variations have been described as two sets of ten, each divided into two sets of five. The overall shape of each five is a kind of ABA where the first and last pair are closely connected in figuration and style, while the middle variation is independent. Listeners less conscious of form, however, will probably find more immediate the control of tension and relaxation. It rises gradually to a climax, releases and rises again, the second time running directly into the fugue. This is not a question of dynamics or clever build-up of registration but the effect of the musical patterns of each variation, of tension within the music. The whole piece is without peer in its sense of dynamic organisation. Even a Neapolitan sixth can never sound as well as it does at the end of this fugue; theoretically the effect is ordinary, but in its context the chord is magnificent.

Organ Sonatas

The usual English name 'Organ Trio Sonatas' describes perfectly well what these pieces are. The trio technique – 1 right hand, 2 left hand, 3 pedal – is an obvious one for organ; it had long been traditional and is to be found in many forms elsewhere in the composer's work. Although three-part organ *fugues* may never have been a very feasible texture, a three-part chorale prelude is, especially if one of the three parts holds the cantus firmus. Every French organ-composer of Bach's period and earlier had written pieces requiring three distinct and differently coloured keyboards including pedal, and some of them have the makings of fully developed trio movements; but in their position as Mass interludes, hymn-preludes or variations, they have been left as miniatures. What distinguishes Bach's trios, apart from their general musical mastery and beauty, is their form: complete sonatas, mostly in three movements, in this fact alone resembling no other organ-music of their period. They are much like those written for other instruments – not so much the violin-and-harpsichord or flute-and-harpsichord sonatas of Bach as the first and last of the three for viola da gamba and harpsichord, BWV 1027 and 1029. Indeed, at least one trio piece, perhaps one of the very 'single trio movements which are to be found here and there' according to Forkel, is known in three versions: one for two flutes and figured bass (BWV 1039, last movement), one for gamba and harpsichord (BWV 1027, last movement) and one for solo organ (BWV 1027a). Although it is not known whether the two-flute version is, as usually thought, older than the gamba version, it does seem that the organ movement was an arrangement from one or other. BWV 1027a is a good, indeed very charming, organ trio-sonata movement, like the others 'written in such *galant* style' that it 'still sounds very good', in the words of the 1788 Comparison between Bach and Handel.[1] Yet the sonatas for organ are different from those for other instruments in important respects. The two upper parts are *always* in dialogue form, whereas the instrumental sonatas have passages or movements in which the harpsichord is purely accompanimental. And while most last movements are fugal in both the organ and the other sonatas, the three-movement plan itself is more consistent in the organ sonatas.

What were the sonatas written for? It could well be that the set was *compiled* (*aufgesetzt*) for W. F. Bach and 'helped him to become the great player he was', as Forkel reported. The complete autograph manuscript has been dated 1727–9, when Friedemann was 17–19, and a further copy, partly in his hand, was made from this source, perhaps before he went to Dresden as organist in 1733 or even before he became a law student in 1729. Such secular-didactic purpose would explain the sonatas' form as chamber-music works; if performed on a chamber organ or a pedal clavichord, the most likely registration would be I 8', II 8', Pedal 8' or 16'. Nevertheless, only one of the six sonatas as they appear in the compilation has an apparently straightforward history. The second movements of nos. 2 and 5, first and third of no. 2 and perhaps all three movements of nos. 3 and 4, were written some time beforehand. The slow movement of no. 3 appears in a transposed and enriched version in the Triple Concerto (BWV 1044); the opening double-movement of no. 4 appears earlier in the same key as a trio for gamba, oboe d'amore and continuo introducing Part II of Cantata 76 (1723); and the opening thirteen bars of the last movement of no. 4 were a possible interlude between the prelude and the fugue of BWV 541. What is interesting is not so much that Bach made more than one version of certain movements but that he did so in such varying guises – solo sonata, triple concerto, organ prelude and fugue, cantata for large forces. Other movements, for example the third of no. 5, may have been originally written for other instruments. No doubt, too, that Mozart was not the only composer of the century to arrange some

[1] David and Mendel, *op. cit.*, p. 285.

movements for string trio. On the other hand, the slow movement of no. 5 is thought to be an original organ piece, written perhaps in the late Weimar period and in some copies placed between the Prelude and Fugue in C (BWV 545). It is difficult to make generalisations from the one trio that does appear to have been a new, integral work, namely no. 6. Even the binary form of the newly composed slow movements (nos. 1 and 6) is also to be found in that of no. 3 – perhaps a sign that the concerto version of this movement was made from the organ version and not vice versa.

Certain details of composition are striking. Although the left hand does not go below tenor C, the three-part texture is generally more evenly spaced than in the classical Italian string trio sonata, and while the upper parts move in mutual imitation, the pedal in some movements (e.g. the third of no. 2) rises to thematic equality. The pedal part does not begin movements with the theme and often needs to simplify its outlines for ease of playing. It is also unable to take many of the running basses and scale-figures that characterise the bass lines of instrumental sonatas; conversely, some movements (e.g. the third of no. 1) have a bass line unlikely ever to have been written for 'cello. For many players it is not so much the agility required of the pedals that is difficult:

Ex. 16
BWV 528 (third movement, bar 60)

43

as the 'independence of thought' necessary to play three contrapuntally self-contained lines:

Ex. 17
BWV 529 (bar 28)

Like the Four Duets (BWV 802–5), such textures are perfect models for the contrapuntists; but it should not be forgotten that the trios also contain very lovely slow-movement themes, a sparkling vivacity in the quick movements unusual even for Bach, and in both quick and slow movements a gift for fluent and original sequences that is matched only by the composer's willingness now and then to drop all harmonic involvements and enjoy simple, concerto-like repetitions of a simple chord:

Ex. 18
BWV 526 (bar 38)

At the same time, some of the movements are very good examples of developed concerto ritornello form, and such movements as the first of no. 1 compare with some Brandenburg Concerto movements in their creation of episodes derived from the main theme. Scarcely a bar of the first movement of Sonata I is without the rising triadic figure announced in bar 1; it is given various forms (straight or inverted) and keys (long supertonic episode in the middle), it appears in imitation and in sequence, it can lead to further melody and it combines with its countersubjects in such a way that either can appear on top. Yet the whole has a bewitching melodic ease and a prettiness of texture that only narrowness of outlook can describe as outside a 'truly idiomatic organ style', in the words of one recent biographer.

Other Leipzig Work

Because the fugue of the Prelude and Fugue in D minor (BWV 539) is known in a simpler version for solo violin in G minor (BWV 1001), it has been customary to call it a 'later arrangement'. There is also a version of the same piece for lute (BWV 1000), but nobody knows for certain who made either the organ or the lute versions. It is perfectly reasonable to suppose that other violin movements of the Köthen period, notably the fugues from sonatas in A minor (BWV 1003) and C major (BWV 1005), were also known to some organists, since such Italianate subjects were recommended at that time by influential writers like Mattheson and Heinichen. The manual prelude of BWV 539 could have been written by anybody superficially versed in French *plein jeu* interludes, although this is no reason to attempt to enliven it by dotting the quavers and creating *notes inégales*, in my opinion. The organ fugue has more imitative parts than the violin version, becoming in its fuller form a successful organ piece, none the worse for its unusually staccato countersubject and simple episodes.

Despite this piece, it is an exaggeration to see arrangements as particularly characteristic of the Leipzig years. Although the Aria in F (BWV 587), for instance, has long been known as an arrangement of an instrumental trio by Couperin in *Les Nations* (Paris, 1726) there is little to suggest that Bach was the arranger, except a late ascription to that effect. Much the same could be said of Telemann's movement arranged as the G major Trio (BWV 586), although this fits better into the Weimar/Leipzig context. More important is that the composer revised older music of his own and made collections of both new and old pieces for publication or preservation.

A difficult question is why Bach wrote organ music after he left Weimar and ceased to be a church organist. The trios were very likely compiled as practice-music: a conventional set of six compiled by new movements. Some *manualiter* chorales were written for Wilhelm Friedemann ('Wer nur den lieben Gott', BWV 691) and for Anna Magdalena ('Jesu, meine Zuversicht', BWV 728, 1722). The Eighteen Chorales were collected, like Book II of the *Forty-Eight*, for reasons best known to collectors or composers tidying up previous work. *Clavierübung III*, the Schübler Chorales and the Canonic Variations were published and must have aimed at least partly at showing a no doubt uncomprehending world what technical skill really was. While the Schübler pieces are tuneful, even *galant* and 'popular', those of *Clavierübung III* were in theory more useful to professional church organists. At least three of the big preludes and fugues (C minor, BWV 546; B minor, BWV 544; E minor, BWV 548) seem by their mastery to belong to the Leipzig years, as also do revisions such as the C major (BWV 545). But the prelude-and-fugue was apparently less important to a master-organist who may have played the organ only as a teacher, a travelling virtuoso and an expert opening new instruments. Perhaps it appears less important because works (including revisions) have been lost or because the virtuoso organist extemporised. Also, there must have been some justification for the remark in the Obituary that:

despite all this knowledge of the organ, he never enjoyed the good fortune, as he used to point out frequently with regret, of having a really large and beautiful organ at his constant disposal. This fact has robbed us of many beautiful and unknown inventions in organ-playing which he would otherwise have written down and displayed in the form in which he had them in his head.

Forkel, from what evidence is unclear, is more explicit in his description of the music improvised by Bach. If he was playing outside the Service for a group of listeners, he first chose a subject and 'used this theme for a prelude and a fugue, with the full organ'. This is an important remark, considering the complete absence of direct connection between almost all preludes and fugues as we know them, i.e. as normally paired by eighteenth-century copyists.

Then he showed his art of using the stops for a trio, a quartet, etc., always upon the same subject. Afterwards followed a chorale, the melody of which was playfully surrounded in the most diversified manner by the original subject, in three or four parts.

Forkel does not describe further what if anything he specifically means by 'quartet', but it could have been of the Italianate kind with theme and accompaniment (e.g. the *adagio* of the Toccata, Adagio and Fugue in C, BWV 564), or a kind of chorale prelude without chorale theme, or a contrapuntal movement of a type familiar in the French *quatuor à trois claviers*.

Finally the conclusion was made by a fugue, with the full organ, in which either another treatment only of the first subject predominated, or one or (according to its nature) two others were mixed with it.

BWV 537 in C minor was a fugue with two new themes introduced in the middle section: one seems to be derived from the original countersubject, but there is no combination of all three in the manner described by Forkel in his last phrase. The 'St Anne' fugue combines themes but not all three together. Forkel's imagination may have been stronger than his evidence, or perhaps he was referring to the kind of treatment undergone by the theme in the St Anne fugue. That he seems to have been referring to Bach's demonstration before Reinken, which as he knew concerned improvisations on a chorale melody, does not increase confidence in the exactness of his report. Nevertheless, a prelude and fugue would be the most important thing to aim at for any extemporiser, as they are today. An observer at Leipzig in about 1741 noted that Bach began with 'something from the printed or written page' in order to 'set his powers of imagination in motion' which he then let flow in extemporisation.[1] It seems from this to have been not at all expected that a famous virtuoso would play from a book of music.

While most of the great preludes and fugues were written before Bach moved to Leipzig, perhaps as postludes to the Service at Weimar, perhaps as brilliant compositions in their own right, some may well have been composed at Leipzig as others too were copied, revised and perhaps even paired there. Incomplete sources will leave it in doubt to which of these categories a certain prelude and fugue belong. The B minor (BWV 544) exists in a fair copy made by the composer between 1727 (watermark) and about 1740 at the latest (handwriting style); part of the Prelude and Fugue in E minor (BWV 548, 'The Wedge') is also autograph and the paper has the same watermark. But when were they composed? Certain details of style may lead us to guess that they were written before the arias of the *Gloria* of the B minor Mass; but parallels between one branch of composition and another are very hard to make in Bach's works. Even harpsichord music presumed to be roughly contemporary shares few characteristics with organ music. The B minor Prelude and Fugue (BWV 544) has so little in common with the B minor Partita (BWV 831, published in 1735), that one is not demonstrably 'later' than the other. The appoggiatura harmonies of both may be an important common factor, but some of the figuration in the prelude (BWV 544) is more reminiscent of obbligato organ parts in such cantatas as BWV 169 and BWV 170 (1726).

Discrepancies of style between prelude and fugue may also imply different origin. A good example is Prelude and Fugue in C minor (BWV 546), where a magnificent prelude, in form close to some of the maturer da capo cantata arias of Bach, is followed by a fugue formally and texturally much simpler, despite an occasional passage in five parts. Although it is hard to believe that the final bars of the fugue do refer to the opening bars of the prelude, as has been suggested, there is no firm reason on the other hand to assume the fugue is an earlier composition. Contrast between the two appears too deliberate, too complete. Nor is the

---

[1] Pitschel's remarks are vague and do not even refer to Bach by name; see W. Neumann and H-J. Schulze, *Bach Dokumente* II (Leipzig, 1969), p. 397. I am grateful to Dr Schulze for his advice on many points discussed in this book.

simple second fugal episode for manuals alone of itself immature or poor; it is not less worthy than the subsidiary material in the St Anne prelude. But internal evidence is a quicksand, and nobody knows that the St Anne prelude in part or as a whole was not composed years before its publication in 1739.

It is the prelude of BWV 546 that best repays attention. It may well be that its numerical balance was carefully planned, not least because the last episode runs into the final statement somewhat unexpectedly:

opening statement	24 bars + cadence
first episode	24 bars + cadence
middle statement, with part of the fugue episode, in three sections	48 bars + cadence
second episode	23 bars without final cadence
final statement (restatement)	24 bars + cadence

Such planning suggests a concerto ritornello, but the material is not that of a string concerto, nor is any manual-changing really feasible. This is an important, original movement, intensely idiomatic for organ and yet in no sense restricted to the Lutheran organ-gallery. Its composer was a cosmopolitan.

The prelude in B minor (BWV 544) has a form fairly similar to that in C minor (BWV 546), but there is not the same clear-cut recapitulation, and the episode material may be seen as more uniform in style with the main theme. The whole is a series of rising and falling sequences, sometimes based on simple harmonies, sometimes on rich chords incorporating harmonic appoggiaturas, many of which are written out as notes of ordinary length, as in some of the composer's harpsichord music of the period. Like Beethoven, Bach was aware of the musical potential of running scales and scale-segments. The fugue too includes running motifs: both a slow quaver theme without leaps and also flowing semiquavers that accompany it throughout in unobtrusive, totally non-Italianate counterpoint. Other figures are introduced and the episodes seem contrived specifically to throw the plain theme into relief. Like certain other fugues, it reaches its final cadence without any rhetorical drawing-out of material; the two-bar phrase has not been allowed to dominate all else in the fugue, as it easily could have done. But the final section contains five such phases bringing a sense of period and finality.

With the 'Wedge' Prelude and Fugue (BWV 548) the player has

perhaps reached the peak of organ-music: an 'organ symphony in two movements' (Spitta) based again on scale motifs, appoggiatura harmonies and many motifs familiar from much earlier music. The prelude is again the more tightly organised of the two movements; the episodes of its ritornello form are derived from the opening theme and only a sequential passage or two are allowed to let the tension fall a little. The fugue episodes are more drawn out, but despite its length of 231 bars the whole is held together both by an unusual formal organisation and by adopting shorter notes for the harmonically simple passages. The fugue is a unique ABA movement, in which the opening exposition is exactly repeated (with extra harmonies at the first bars of return) after a middle section. This middle section is not only precisely twice as long as the opening in terms of bar-numbers, but becomes increasingly tense as it moves towards the da capo repeat. The C minor fugue (BWV 537) had reached towards this shape, but its middle section was itself divided into two large paragraphs. The conception of the Wedge Fugue is grand and startling. As in other long fugues (such as the three-part *ricercare* in the *Musical Offering* or the *fuga* of the C major Violin Sonata) the composer seems to be deliberately walking a tightrope in the Wedge Fugue by interpolating extra material, sharply differentiating episode from entry, controlling it with great tension, yet at the same time giving it a feeling of unplanned caprice and 'inspiration'. He achieves all this in the Wedge and *Musical Offering* fugues not least by the melodic power of the theme itself. Very few of his fugues follow the book, especially when their themes are so strong in character and beautiful in themselves.

Clavierübung III

In 1740 Lorenz Mizler, former pupil of Bach, noted that in *Clavierübung III*, then recently issued, 'the composer has published further proof that in this kind of music he has more excellent experience and fortune than many others. No one will improve on him in this sphere and very few will be able to imitate him'.[1] Such encomiums were helpful not so much to local musicians as to those who had heard of the composer only by

[1] Neumann and Schulze, *op. cit.*, p. 387.

repute: for *Clavierübung III* was Bach's first published organ music.

Almost all the pieces are known only from this edition, and it is assumed – but only assumed – that they were written near the date of publication. Two engravers worked on it, one imitating the composer's own handwriting (hence the suggestion that the St Anne prelude was engraved by Bach himself), the other not.[1] Two staves are used for all pieces except the bigger chorales (BWV 676, 678, 682, 686). The price of three *Reichstaler* must have been high for organists, since a clavichord at that time in Saxony could have cost no more than twenty *Taler*. There are twenty-seven pieces, including the opening Prelude, the closing Fugue ('St Anne', BWV 552) and what are almost certainly four independent harpsichord pieces (the *Vier Duetten*, BWV 802–5). The number 3 is prominent – Clavierübung Vol. 3, 27 pieces ($3 \times 3 \times 3$), three flat key-signatures of the framing pieces, three sections in the final fugue – and many admirers have seen here references to the Trinity; but a similar list could also be made of numbers 2 and 4 in different connections.

The full title is *Third Part of KEYBOARD PRACTICE containing various preludes on Catechism-hymns and others, for the organ. Composed by Johann Sebastian Bach for the spiritual refreshment of music-lovers and particularly connoisseurs of such work.* Thus the common English label 'German Organ Mass' is misleading, since more is concerned than the Lutheran Missa Brevis of *Kyrie* and *Gloria*, and there is no question of its being an organ mass in the sense of the *messes pour l'orgue*. The chorales on which the first *Clavierübung* preludes are based were sung at the beginning of the Leipzig *Hauptgottesdienst* (main Sunday Service) and it is reasonable to assume that the composer intended them as Service pieces for Lutheran organists: a repertory to choose from rather than a single cycle. There are indeed two 'cycles' of preludes as there are also two Lutheran Catechisms, a large and a small. For organs without pedals (rare in Saxony) or for organists without pedal-technique (less rare – perhaps the music-lovers or 'amateurs' referred to in the title), each chorale has a setting for manual only, not at all easy to play but relatively small in scale. As pairs or, in the case of the *Gloria* hymn, a trio of settings, the preludes offer examples of many very varied techniques. The device of decorated

[1] The latter was Balthasar Schmid of Nuremberg, publisher of the Goldberg Variations and Canonic Variations.

melody above accompaniment is not met here, as it is in the *Eighteen* or *Orgelbüchlein*, but the remaining chorale-prelude devices are explored most imaginatively. This variety has already been referred to in connection with the Lord's Prayer chorale 'Vater unser im Himmelreich'.

They must surely have been unusual connoisseurs who had their spirits refreshed by the larger settings in *Clavierübung III*. However one views Scheibe's famous attack on Bach in 1737, those who agreed with him would have found two years later plenty of evidence for the opinion that he

> deprived his pieces of that which was natural, giving them a bombastic and confused character and eclipsing their beauty by too much art.[1]

It is an argument sometimes difficult to refute, for the very mastery has a forbidding air and the several organ styles were almost unsympathetically old-fashioned – just at the period when Bach himself seems to have sensed the *galanterie* of the new music, judging by the arias written for the Mass in B minor or those arranged for the Christmas Oratorio a few years before *Clavierübung III* was published. Some of the settings seem to have only a tenuous connection with the text. The 'wrath of God' and 'hellish pain' of the text may be dimly seen in the exuberant, wide-stretching figures of 'Jesus Christus unser Heiland' (BWV 688), but it is easier to believe that the composer was more interested in finding faultless invertible counterpoint to the pedal chorale theme – contrapuntal lines which are in many ways equally (or even more) suitable for string instruments. It is possible to imagine the composer reacting to a chorale melody and its text in other than graphic ways. We cannot know why a certain musical figure sprang to mind, whether there was an unconscious reference to a particular word or to the general mood of the text, or how a musical motif is related to anything but itself. It is the indefinable nature of 'inspiration' that is at issue throughout Bach's career as a composer of organ chorales, something that effectively prevents us from ever knowing the working of this or any composer's mind – or even how much he was relying on tradition, on musical devices familiar to other and older organists.

Although the title itself, *Clavierübung*, was not Bach's invention for collections of music, there is an undeniably monumental

[1] Neumann and Schulze, *op. cit.*, p. 286.

originality about planning a set of preludes introduced and rounded off by a great prelude and fugue. The St Anne Prelude and Fugue (BWV 552) is not like any other pair in the whole corpus. The prelude is Bach's longest, and is built up of three ideas: the opening dotted *ouverture* rhythm, a staccato crotchet motif with echoes, and a running semiquaver bass. All three are quite different from each other, and although the length makes it a difficult piece to perform convincingly – the undistinguished *quasi galant* second theme seems to require a quicker tempo than the other two – the conspicuous character of each makes for a movement formally interesting to follow in one's mind or on paper. Despite elements from both French *ouverture* and Italian *concerto*, the piece is unique. The fugue, stylistically and tonally worlds away from the movement in *Clavierübung III* which precedes it – the fourth Duetto – is a splendid example of the old cumulative fugue whose sections are based either on different versions of the same subject or on secondary subjects which combine with the first. Its three sections may 'represent' the persons of the Trinity, as has been suggested, but from Frescobaldi's period to Buxtehude's the arrangement had yielded good results and there is no need to find extra-musical parallels. The very opening theme had traditional associations. The first section exploits five-part Italianate counterpoint, one of the virtues of this style being that when it is well done the theme has a curiously different effect each time it enters; the second drops the pedal and runs as countersubject to the theme now converted into triple time, like some of Frescobaldi's; the third introduces the running semiquavers so characteristic of the composer. The theme now appears syncopated, spacious and almost ostinato.

The chorale-settings follow the E flat prelude in Lutheran order: *Kyrie–Christe–Kyrie* (2 settings each), *Gloria* (3), Ten Commandments (2), *Credo* (2), Lord's Prayer (2), Baptism (2), Penitence (2), Communion (2). The old 'motet' style of chorale-prelude writing immediately appears; three massive movements in 4/2, with Italianate counterpoint, imitative entries based on the first line of the melody, ponderous themes and long-note cantus firmus melodies successively in treble, tenor and bass. As a trio of pieces they have a style like previous *Kyrie* settings (e.g. *Kyrie II* from the B minor Mass) but are difficult in concert performance. One ingenious idea for registration is to leave out all manual reeds (which few organists of Bach's period had anyway) for the first two preludes, drawing a pedal reed only for the third, where the theme goes into the bass and cuts through the counterpoint like old French cantus firmus interludes. The big chorales may also be interspersed with the smaller *manualiter* settings. These are short, lighter fughetta movements with irregular entries but with a striking fluency. The fughetta too was an old form, one used earlier by many composers including Bach himself. The triple, compound and compound-triple time of the three pieces assures different musical effects: the chorale melodies have become more liquescent, and all the triple time gives no end of opportunity for those seeking musical symbolisms.

The longer setting of the *Gloria* hymn 'Allein Gott in der Höh' ' (BWV 676) is not dissimilar in technique: a long strict trio, nearly three times as long as the so-called Weimar version (BMV 676a), incorporating both the chorale theme and paraphrases on it running from manual to manual. The first of the smaller settings is a two-part invention weaving fluid triplets around the notes of a theme left intact in an inner voice. The other setting (BWV 677) is a little fugue demonstrably built on, but carefully disguising, the same theme. Three settings, all in three parts.

The Ten Commandments preludes offer scope for conjecture. One is a long development of the cantus firmus in octave canon *en taille* (in the middle), the other a lively fughetta on the paraphrased theme. Canon = law = Commandments; the wandering upper voices suggest the aimless meander of feeble man, as they do in 'Vater unser' (BWV 682); the whole of BWV 678 can be seen as containing ten subdivisions; the fughetta (BWV 679) has ten entries of a subject encompassing ten semitones (g–f). Of course the chorale theme was particularly open to canonic treatment, judging by other settings of it in Cantata 77 and in the *Orgelbüchlein*. Whether the theme's associations were so strong that a musical-symbolic point is made in Cantata 77 even without the text (the canon appears there on instruments only) is doubtful, to say the least. And some may think that a musical portrait of the aimless meanderings of amoral man steers uncomfortably near the dangers of the Intentional Fallacy. What is more immediate is the strength of the following fugue, 'Wir glauben all' ' (BWV 680), based on the theme of the *Credo* and supported by a quasi ostinato pedal striding confidently below. Such counterpoint is essentially Italianate, and striking is the complete change of style in the smaller setting of the chorale; here the fughetta is based on the theme now Frenchified in rhythm and thus changed beyond recognition. The little jerky runs and dramatic rests make it a fine harpsichord piece, as do the smoother, beautifully integrated runs of the lesser of the preludes on 'Vater unser im Himmelreich' (BWV 683).

The greater prelude on 'Vater unser' (BWV 682) offers yet more insight into the potential of the organ chorale. At once the most complicated and longest in time of Bach's chorales, 'Vater unser' is also the most difficult to play well. Its combination of staccato triplets and legato snapped rhythms (which are only written-out appoggiaturas typical of the composer's mature style) results in the language of a player, not a listener. To the composer the problem here, as in BWV 678, was to make a satisfactory form from a canon in long notes (cantus firmus at the fifth), singing its way through the middle of an intricate trio-sonata movement that is itself based on the chorale theme and exploits imitation. The piece may well be thought to be more integrated and interesting than BWV 678, however, not least because of the more distinguished motifs and a more interestingly obsessive pedal part. The relationship of canon to other parts may be explained in the same way as BWV 678, and one commentator has gone so far as to see the prelude as picturing successively the evils listed in Luther's Catechism hymn: false teaching, the wrath of Satan, resistance to God's will, strife, guilt, evil spirit, evil times. For those less confident about knowing the frame of mind of any mid-eighteenth-century German Lutheran composer, the chief interest of the piece may be its position in Bach's canonic output and the hints it gives of the later pieces that explore hair-raising difficulties of technique.

In comparison, the pieces on the baptismal 'Christ unser Herr zum Jordan kam' are straightforward: the first, a two-part invention for right hand above a running line probably paraphrasing the same chorale-melody that appears in long pedal notes, and the second, a three-part fughetta with inverted answer and a derivative subject. Both versions may be presumed to refer to the flowing Jordan, although how these running semiquavers differ in implication from those of 'Allein Gott in der Höh'' is not at all obvious. The 'Aus tiefer Noth' preludes are also a typical *Clavierübung* pair, the first a big 'motet' piece with slow,

vocal lines, the second a three-part fughetta that also incorporates
the cantus firmus in the upper part – something unusual in
manualiter chorales, though also found in BWV 675. The big
'Aus tiefer Noth' is a grand climax of the 'motet' chorales, one of
the few six-part pieces in organ music and the only known example
by Bach, except for what the 1788 Comparison between Bach and
Handel called 'a fugue on the Royal Prussian theme for six voices
manualiter' (Ricercare à 6, *The Musical Offering*). The contrapuntal
language is conventional of its type, but little dactyl rhythms
increase towards the end and dissolve the forbidding grandeur.
It is such keyboard devices that help to distinguish the style from
the true vocal polyphony it pretends to be imitating, as can be
seen by comparing BWV 686 with the choral setting of the same
hymn in Cantata 38.

Ex. 19

(i) Cantata 38 (vocal parts)

(ii) BWV 686

Most of the so-called 'motet-style' organ chorales have livelier textures than their vocal equivalents and perhaps ought to be called something else.

The final pair of organ chorales comprises a manual invention above the pedal melody (BWV 688) and a fughetta for manuals, here labelled *Fuga* because it is more fully worked out (BWV 689). The latter is a fugue not out of keeping with some of the *Forty-Eight*, despite the thematic augmentation near the end which closely approaches the chorale. Both BWV 688 and 678 give the manuals a theme independent of the chorale, while BWV 684 has largely independent upper parts. The inventing of a totally new melody was an important feature: long known in many of the cantatas incorporating a cantus firmus movement, it rarely occurred in organ music. Those chorales with new melodies in the Schübler preludes were arrangements from such cantatas.

The remaining movements in *Clavierübung III* – those separating the last organ chorale from the St Anne fugue – are the *Vier Duetten* (BWV 802–5): models of invertible counterpoint and tonal organisation known to many students but rarely played by organists. Are they organ-music? Were the *Vier Duetten* slipped into Vol. III of the *Clavierübung* to make it convenient for the printer? Or perhaps to make up the twenty-seven pieces? They are not mentioned on the title-page, and J. Elias Bach had already in January 1739 described the forthcoming publication as some *Clavier pieces* 'mainly' (not only?) for organists.[1] In performance, the duets can be integrated with the chorale-preludes, interspersing the smaller settings which, though also written for pedal-less keyboard instrument, are conceived quite differently. The *Bach-*

[1] Neumann and Schulze, *op. cit.*, p. 335.

Jahrbuch (1949–50) contains an ingenious demonstration by Klaus Ehricht that the duets are related melodically to some of the earlier preludes in *Clavierübung III*, but resemblances are never hard to find – the triadic imitation of no. 2, for example, is reminiscent of other pieces elsewhere in F major. Because the duets are in two parts, the spacing and relative tessitura are different enough from any authentic organ piece to invalidate easy comparison. In nos. 1, 2 and 3 especially, the bass-line scarcely has a note that could not serve in the upper part, so equal is the counterpoint. The invertibility of the two duet parts is another facet of Bach's increasing interest in canon and genuine melodic counterpoint void of Italianate formulas. At the same time, there is in nos. 1, 2 and 4 a noticeable character of melodic chromaticism not different from certain new *galant* traits current then in central Germany, except that it is better done. In short, what the pieces are is uncertain; but no harpsichordist could doubt that they belong to his instrument.

Schübler Chorale Preludes

It is not possible to say whether it was actually the set of six Schübler preludes that was responsible for a style of chorale-prelude popular amongst central German organists in the later eighteenth century or whether Bach was merely indicating a trend – probably the latter. The set was published in 1746 or later by J. G. Schübler, a former pupil of the composer, and sold by the publisher, the composer and 'the latter's sons in Berlin and Halle', i.e. C. P. E. and W. F. Bach. Five are known to be untransposed arrangements of cantata movements which incorporate the melody concerned:

'Wachet auf!' (BWV 645), Cantata 140 (1731), tenor aria
'Wer nur den lieben Gott' (BWV 647), Cantata 93 (1724), duet for soprano & alto
'Meine Seele erhebt den Herrn' (BWV 648), Cantata 10 (1724), duet for alto & tenor
'Ach bleib' bei uns' (BWV 649), Cantata 6 (1725), soprano aria
'Kommst du nun, Jesu' (BWV 650), Cantata 137 (1725), alto aria

Four are trios, two are in four parts; the pedal part is left as a plain bass and the basso continuo harmonies of the cantata versions are not realised. The sixth prelude, 'Wo soll ich fliehen hin' (BWV 646) could well be an original organ piece, as its figurations do not immediately suggest any other instrument or colour; but the left-hand part looks, and is registered to sound, like a basso continuo complete with double bass at 16' pitch.

The style of the Schübler preludes is essentially different from the other collections, reflecting as it does their vocal origins and, as a published work, perhaps the desire to be immediately appealing. With the exception of BWV 646 and perhaps 647, the style is tuneful and the melodic character unusual for organ pieces. Yet they are not simply 'arrangements'. Each prelude has the chorale-theme as a cantus firmus line, and most have their own melody – one basically independent of the chorale theme, even if initially derived from it, like BWV 649. The result is a melodious counterpoint, not imitative, without Italian formulas: a kind of counterpoint that really is a combination of two themes instead of pretending to be so. The counterpoint of an Italian piece by Bach can be usefully compared with one of the Schübler preludes:

Ex. 20

(i) BWV 589

Ped.

(ii) BWV 645 (bar 13)

Ped.

While the former has all the devices typical of Italian alla breve counterpoint – suspensions, contrary motion, a carefully gauged line moving when the other is stationary or leaping when the other moves by step – the latter approaches closer the ideal of two genuinely independent melodies, each a theme in its own right, each fit to be heard without the other. Each line of the first example relies for its effect on the other, and neither is in fact 'independent' at all. In all the Schübler preludes the 'new theme' returns ritornello-like between lines of the chorale, often over-lapping and cleverly giving the impression that the chorale theme need not be there, that the piece is already a self-contained ritornello movement. Close study of, for instance, BWV 650 will reveal that the 'new melody' does not entirely go its own way and that the composer has very clearly manipulated it to combine in part with the chorale theme, in part not. BWV 645 and 649 (where the original cantata obbligato instrument was a violoncello piccolo) are further examples of this technique, BWV 648 perhaps the best of all from this point of view.

Exactly how the preludes relate to their chorale texts is difficult to say, although many players feel they understand a connection. Very often in the music of Bach the flash of understanding has to be experienced personally, even privately, and cannot be induced by a second person. Even though the fleeting figures and syn-copations of 'Wo soll ich fliehen hin' ('Where shall I fly?') may suggest hasty motion, its alternative title and text 'Auf meinen lieben Gott' ('In need and anxiety I put my trust in God') suggest something more measured and stolid. Presumably the first was the text referred to, and comparison with the same melody used in a cantata ('Ich habe meine Zuversicht', BWV 188) gives yet another, different idea of the melody. Nevertheless, another setting of 'Wo soll ich fliehen hin' in the Kirnberger collection (BWV 694) uses similar motifs and its greater length encourages a completely fluid interpretation of the non-stop semiquavers. The settings represent the action of flight rather than the eventual succour implied in the title-question.

Canonic Variations,'Vom Himmel Hoch' (BWV 769)

According to Lorenz Mizler, founder of the Leipzig Society for the Musical Sciences and editor of the music journal containing the original Obituary of the composer, the Society received J. S. Bach as a member in 1747 – a musician not noted for his theoretical speculations – whereupon he presented 'the chorale "Vom Himmel hoch da komm' ich her" completely worked out'. This is taken to refer to the Canonic Variations, the phrase 'completely worked out' being an apt description of a five-part partita containing canons at the octave, fifth, sixth, seventh, third, second, ninth, inverted, augmented, in diminution, in stretto and in combination at least twice with the notes BACH.

Canonic treatment – in sections rather than whole works – had long been common in chorale settings, and either the theme or its accompaniment could supply the canonic parts. In three of these five canons, the accompanying parts begin as derivations of the theme itself. It is possible that the little three-bar *canon triplex à 6 voc.* included in the portrait Bach presented to Mizler's Society gave the idea for the 'Vom Himmel hoch' variations, as its bass bears some resemblance to the chorale melody. Previous preludes based on the melody (BWV 700, 701, 738) suggested motifs open to highly imitative treatment, BWV 701 (also in C major) already combining the different chorale lines harmonically. Whether or not anything specifically Christmas-like can be heard in the music is uncertain, though the first canon has figurations exuberant enough to match such pieces as the canonic Advent prelude 'Gottes Sohn ist kommen' in the *Orgelbüchlein* (BWV 600). Perhaps the strangest circumstance surrounding the Canonic Variations is that Bach published them not only at about the same time as the utterly different Schübler chorales – as if to earn approval of both musical philosophers and musical practitioners – but that he published them partially unrealised. For all their complex jugglings, the first three canons are not written out, and while some organists may have been able to read the original open-score version of Variation 4 (with its four different clefs), nobody could have found it easy to fill in the unwritten canon in Variation 2:

Ex. 21

Like the *Musical Offering* and parts of the *Art of Fugue*, the published version cannot be used for a performing edition as it stands.

The two extant versions of the *Canonic Variations* – autograph manuscript and printed edition, both dating from the last years of the composer's life – raise an interesting question of order for the pieces. Certain details in each variation differ from one version to the other (especially in the Canon at the Seventh); the canons are written out completely in the manuscript version; and the order printed (Canon at the Octave, Fifth, Seventh, Augmented, Inverted) is different from the order in the manuscript (Canon at the Octave, Fifth, Inverted, Seventh, Augmented). Few people are certain that they know the composer's final wishes in the matter, but the printed order is the one most often followed, presumably because the final bars give a climactic, six-part combination of all four lines of the chorale in stretto, closing with the BACH motif, and all based on a pedal point – 'completely worked out', as was said. But the manuscript version has this movement as the central of the five – a reasonable position for the most varied movement in a set of canons. It may or may not be a coincidence that the *Musical Offering*, whose printed order is much more confused and for different reasons, was published with its biggest movement (the six-part Ricercare) followed by smaller canons.

The Eighteen Chorale-Preludes

Custom has made 'The Eighteen' a familiar title for the collection of chorale-preludes (BWV 651–668) composed at Weimar but copied and revised in Leipzig at the end of Bach's life. However, the *Neue Bach Ausgabe* has confirmed that 'The Seventeen' would be a more suitable title since in the mostly autograph copy the eighteenth ('Vor deinem Thron', BWV 668) does not follow the seventeenth. Between the two come the complete Canonic Variations (BWV 769). All the eighteen have earlier known versions from the Weimar period. Two melodies have two different settings, a further two have three settings. All were copied very late, perhaps in part as late as 1749; nos. 16 and 17 were copied or added by Altnikol for unknown reasons; no. 18 was copied by 'one of his friends' as the composer's eyesight was failing, according to a prefatory note in *The Art of Fugue* which may refer to this manuscript. The whole collection serves as a particularly good example of Bach's reworking methods – collecting older material at Leipzig, arranging or revising it into groups of pieces.

The Eighteen do not have the immediate expressiveness of the *Orgelbüchlein* or the striking melodiousness of some of the Schübler; in many ways the collection seems more closely related to *Clavierübung III*, as one might expect. On the other hand it is not surprising to find the part-writing less consistent than that of the *Orgelbüchlein*, which from a technical point of view is a very remarkable collection.[1] The seventeen preludes (BWV 651–667) were fair-copied, and more than hint at a cyclic arrangement which worsening health probably prevented from being completed. The first and last piece, both of which address the Holy Ghost, are registered *organo pleno*. Neither BWV 651 nor 667 was so marked in their earlier and much shorter Weimar version, while one that was originally so marked (no. 15, BWV 665) has been re-marked *sub communione* instead. A complete liturgical plan does not readily suggest itself, but this registration alone might hint at an arrangement not dissimilar to *Clavierübung III*, not least in that no. 11 (BWV 661) is also marked *organo pleno* like the central fugue of *Clavierübung III* ('Wir glauben all' ', BWV 680).

While comparison of the Weimar and Leipzig versions of a prelude does lead to some understanding of the composer's approaches, perhaps even more important is that the collection offers examples – all extensive and thoroughly worked out – of many varied chorale-prelude types. Once again, variety in the techniques of composition seems to have been a guiding principle of the collection. One commentator sees there three trios, five coloratura pieces, three with the theme in the pedal, three in imitative Pachelbel style, one with a 4' pedal and three movements of a descriptive kind; another sees there six decorated cantus firmus preludes with the theme in treble or tenor (BWV 653, 654, 659, 660, 662, 663), two mighty fantasias (BWV 651, 661), two virtuoso trios (BWV 655, 664), three preludes with initial

[1] The *Orgelbüchlein* was copied almost entire in *c*. 1740 by an unknown hand (once thought to be Kirnberger, who may have been a pupil between 1739 and 1741), and includes the revised version of 'Christus der uns selig macht' (BWV 620).

imitation for each line of the hymn (BWV 652, 657, 668), and so on. In all the collections of organ chorales Bach took over historical types (for instance, the sectional prelude with initial imitation, in Pachelbel's style) and then developed away from the old formulae into new melodic lines and melody-types. The very length of most of the Eighteen results in a kind of remoteness, but at least some of them like 'Schmücke dich' (BWV 654) inspired Schumann and many others before and since to great enthusiasm.

The collection begins with an immense fantasia on 'Komm, heiliger Geist' (BWV 651), a piece twice as long as its Weimar version and developing imitative points, episodes, and subsidiary motifs that return. The whole is based on the cantus firmus theme that appears only after a pedal point. The main motif, that which gives the fluent character to the extended piece and which is effortlessly spun out from bar to bar, is a 'paraphrase' of the first line of the hymn-tune and can be taken as an example of that technique for the several preludes that apply it:

Ex. 22

The next prelude (BWV 652) is also a setting of this melody, again a somewhat longer version of a Weimar prelude. Mood and musical technique are totally different from BWV 651, but one does not have to believe the composer to have been activated solely by a desire for variety. Such a text as 'Come, Holy Ghost' can strike a composer in many ways, and a boisterous setting based on a perpetuum mobile flow of semiquavers might well be followed by a more lyrical, perhaps supplicatory version with the theme turned into a decorative melody:

Ex. 23
BWV 652 (bar 16)

The Holy Ghost can be approached prayerfully or exultantly; the Whitsuntide Holy Ghost seems to dance in the *Orgelbüchlein* jig (BWV 631), later extended in the Eighteen (BWV 667) to contain a second verse of rushing tongues-of-fire above the pedal theme. Reconciling Gregorian chant, jig rhythm and pedal syncopations in BWV 631/667 is a problem to delight the player.

The collection contains at least six examples of each type shown in Ex. 22 and Ex. 23 respectively – the so-called 'paraphrase prelude' in BWV 651, 655, 656, 657, 664, 665 and the 'decorative melody prelude' in BWV 652, 653, 654, 659, 660, 662, 663. Many preludes begin with imitation of various kinds, with or without pedal, based on lines either free or derived from the melody. The paraphrase technique of 'Allein Gott in der Höh'' (BWV 664) is so thoroughly developed, compared with the other setting of the melody in BWV 663, that the unadorned cantus firmus melody appears only at bar 85 of the 96-bar prelude. A bubbling, non-stop figuration characterises both BWV 663 and 664, and is suitable for the *Gloria* text and chorale; BWV 662 is a more meditative setting, the theme a decorative melody, like the accompaniment rich in ornaments, pretty figurations and a harmonic style close to the *Orgelbüchlein*. The three settings of 'Nun komm' der Heiden Heiland' (BWV 659–661), a melody well known from the Advent cantatas, are equally varied: (i) an ornamental melody, (ii) a strict and livelier trio, and (iii) one of the *organo pleno* fantasias with theme in the pedal. Despite the unusually low tessitura of the second, it is the first which probably leaves the strongest impression: one of the beautiful chorale preludes, with a melody of characteristic tenderness and smooth, natural inner parts using few of the formulae readily available to an organ-composer. Like Buxtehude in many of his preludes, Bach adds a pedal point at the end with a lovely, soaring melody above in the right hand, as if the melody left the chorale-theme and went its own way.

The effect of such pieces, as of 'Schmücke dich', is completely original, however traditional were some of the techniques involved. Were they to be performed during the Service, one cannot help suspecting that at least some of the congregation would have failed to recognise the theme, however familiar. The decorations surrounding the theme of 'Nun komm'' must have disguised any melody; in 'Schmücke dich' the very drawing out of the melody into long notes effectively changes its character. The long notes of the same chorale in the opening chorus of Cantata 180 are of course more recognisable since they have the words with them; nor are they in any case as long drawn-out as those of BWV 654. It could well be this quality of unhurried, almost indulgent confidence in the texture and patterns of sound created that caused Schumann to think BWV 654 'as priceless, deep and full of soul as any piece of music that ever sprang from a true artist'.

Not all the Eighteen reach these heights, and variety of technique sometimes appears to be the only aim. Interpreters may find in the chorale text a reason why the three-verse setting 'O Lamm Gottes unschuldig' (BWV 656) has two verses for manuals only (the first with the theme in the treble, the second in the alto, the third in the pedal), and it may be possible to see a textual reason for the obvious musical climax in the end of verse three; but the whole seems calculated rather to demonstrate some of the techniques at the organ-composer's disposal. The pedal point at the end is quite undistinguished compared with that in 'Von Gott will ich nicht lassen' (the setting of a theme known to organists as Lebègue's *noël* 'Une vierge pucelle'). At least one pair of settings ('Jesus Christus, unser Heiland', the second copied by Altnikol) seems to have been put in as an equivalent to the contrasted pairs of chorales in *Clavierübung III*. Whether Altnikol did right in including a manual prelude is open to question. The chromatic section of BWV 665 may refer to its text (the pains to be encountered by the Saviour) but can hardly be said to be well integrated in the piece as a whole. Similarly it may well be only the death-bed associations that give 'Vor deinen Thron tret' ich' any special quality, the 'expression of pious resignation and devotion' which Forkel heard in it, or the abstract numerology heard by others.[1] But its shorter, more decorated version in the *Orgelbüchlein* ('Wenn wir in höchsten Nöthen sein') seems to me much more beautiful.

The decoration of the melody 'Vor deinen Thron' in the chorale 'Wenn wir in höchsten Nöthen sein' – chorale preludes using the same tune over the same accompaniment – raises the matter of Bach's notation in organ chorales. It appears from its notation that the version of 'An Wasserflüssen Babylon' in the Eighteen (BWV 653) has more dotted rhythms and more interesting lines than its earlier version (BWV 653a). It appears also that 'Komm heiliger Geist' (BWV 652) is more decorated than the earlier version of the same piece (BWV 652a). But these features do not necessarily imply second thoughts on the composer's part – merely perhaps codified practice, i.e. they reflect what he actually played. It must often have been that even a reasonably imaginative organist would have decorated such pieces. There are moments in organ chorales written throughout the composer's life when either 'set' ornaments (trills, etc.) or 'unset' figurations (free melismas and groups of notes) could be applied with happy

[1] The undecorated version has a first line of 14 notes which can be understood as presenting the name BACH numerologically if $A = 1$, $B = 2$, $C = 3$, $H = 8$ $(1 + 2 + 3 + 8 = 14)$.

results, especially when a line is repeated. 'Ich ruf' zu dir' from the *Orgelbüchlein* is an example; but it is impossible to be over-cautious or over-discreet.

The Art of Fugue

F. W. Marpurg, who wrote the preface to the 1752 edition of the *Art of Fugue*, thought it a special quality of the work that 'every-thing it contains is written in open score' and added that the virtue of this had 'long been unquestionable'. But unquestionable to whom? Like C. P. E. Bach he saw it as a perfect fugal exposé, used perhaps most advantageously along with a good textbook (preferably the one by Marpurg himself), and certainly as 'the most perfect practical fugal work' for teaching purposes. For this reason, open score is useful since it shows 'each voice worked as thoroughly as the others', in Marpurg's opinion. But open-score had also once been familiar in organ music – less familiar no doubt to German organists in the 1750s but at least of a piece with comparable works like the *Musical Offering* and the Canonic Variations. The last is an acknowledged organ-piece; the ricercare of the *Musical Offering* seems to have been planned for two hands and not six separate instruments. Not only does the ricercare agree with the accounts of Bach extemporising a six-part keyboard fugue (on another theme) to the King of Prussia, but it was indeed copied to be played *sull'Org. col Ped. obl.* in a later manuscript by J. F. Agricola, while according to the 1788 Comparison between Bach and Handel the piece was for six voices *manualiter*. Similarly the *Art of Fugue* is often today performed on the organ, very justifiably. The versions differ according to whether the organist breaks off at the point where the engraved edition stops or whether he continues with one or other of the more recent completions. That it was 'Bach's last major work' – a gigantic, unique, incomplete creation – has allowed many to prefer the final fugue incomplete. There is also a tendency to play the series of fugues as if they were solemn, weighty works admitting little variety other than increased volume; when played by string instruments in one or other arrangement, the tendency is to treat them as quiet, sombre works, awesome and remote. But as organ music there is no reason against taking them as strong, vigorous works, calm rather than sombre tense and sustained rather than monotonous.

It is interesting that between autograph and printed edition there is again disagreement over the order of pieces. Even the title may not be the composer's. Some scholars have reasonably questioned whether the final fugue, the incomplete movement built on three themes, belongs at all to the work; without it the longest and most developed movements again occupy a central position in the first printed version of *c.* 1750-1. The two-, three- and four-part textures suit keyboard instruments perfectly well and many arguments have been brought forward to associate the whole work with the organ or harpsichord. The theme in its inverted form (Contrapuncti 3 and 4) also bears some resemblance – some think it an unmistakable resemblance – to the chorale melody 'Aus tiefer Noth' set twice in *Clavierübung III*. It is not a necessary association, but perhaps deserves more than mere rejection since it centres attention on a side of the work so often eclipsed by its gigantic contrapuntal skill: namely, that it has a beauty of its own, in some details of technique not far removed from certain chorale preludes. The pedal often becomes impractical in figuration and compass, and the organist must accept that at least the third mirror canon (BWV 1080, no. 18) is idiomatic harpsichord music, either as a solo or in duet. But none of this affects the essential beauty of the work.

Few if any organists of the 1750s would have found any use for the *Art of Fugue* movements in the Service, and it is not surprising that C. P. E. Bach should advertise in 1756 that 'only about 30 copies' had been disposed of.[1] But for a century or more variation works of many and varied kinds – though certainly not as intricate and independent as the *Art of Fugue* – had been thought of both as private pieces for study and as public pieces for recitals. The late eighteenth- and nineteenth-century heritage of academic fugue-writing should not colour the *Art of Fugue* so much that it becomes confined to the student's library. Fortunately, the work is now performed more and more in organ concert-cycles, though not without some performers allowing themselves to play the unfinished fugue incomplete. There is probably no musical experience so exasperating as sudden silence in bar 240 of the Fugue with Three Subjects.

---

[1] David and Mendel, *op. cit.*, p. 269.

The Organ of J. S. Bach

On no single organ that Bach is known ever to have played would all of his music have sounded at its best. In the first two or perhaps three decades of his life, a sharper, more reverberant north German sound is most often the ideal, but at Mühlhausen and Weimar the instruments at his disposal and therefore influencing his music had a more colourful, less strident southern palette. During the last thirty years of his life, and despite periodic visits to important organs in various towns, he was out of touch with the big instruments embodying the new aesthetic of the 1730s: organs geared towards large sound, crude contrast, smooth reeds, colourful choruses but little real delicacy and subtle piquancy. In many ways, the organs of Bach's main area of activity showed the same kind of influences as his own music: a basic German traditionalism, tempered with French colours and Italian fluency. The best organ-builder of neighbouring Saxony, Gottfried Silbermann (1683–1753), personally typified these influences, being born in Saxony, learning the French art in Alsace, coming into contact with certain Italian sounds, and building in the traditions of central Germany where he finally settled down to work.

An organist playing any instrument in central Germany during, say, the 1720s could be certain of his organ in vital respects. For example, he knew that most of his stops would combine well with others and leave the counterpoint audible. His mechanical action permitted a feeling of intimacy with the sound of the pipes. He could not make an immense or overpowering noise, but he had a huge variety of colour to choose from. If good, his organ had been built by a maker well able to understand the acoustical properties of the church concerned, content to make not a 'factory organ' but one placed, arranged, planned, designed and voiced for that building and its musical (rather than liturgical) demands. If there was more than one manual, the second would speak as directly to the church as the first, and wherever it was placed (at his back, immediately above the music-desk, at the top of the main organ-case, etc.) it would provide a sharp, clear, adequate and colourful contrast to the first – suitable for all chorale preludes, two-manual preludes, trio sonatas, and even fugues.

Bach's generalised registrations in the Schübler preludes – merely specifying pitch, not colour – would have been very useful to German organists whose traditions were less exactly codified than the French, Italian or English. Some of Bach's registration is, like the high pedal part of 'In dulci jubilo' (BWV 608), a notational device rather than a literal direction for combining stops. Thus the registration of Prinzipal 8' (manual) and Trompete 8' (pedal) for 'Gottes Sohn ist kommen' (BWV 600) in the *Orgelbüchlein* may perhaps refer to the Weimar Court chapel organ, but also serves as a reminder to the organist to give the canonic voices a certain pitch-level that would result in their sounding an octave apart. As to how often Bach expected the organist to change manuals, neither extreme position – that he never changed, or that he always changed – is quite tenable. It is possible that even exceptional fugues like the 'Wedge' were played without changing manuals, but until a close comparison is made with the harpsichord music of the Leipzig period, there is little to do but express guesses.

For many pieces, such as the Trios, much indirect evidence suggests that quiet, unglittering combinations of basic stops were the most likely – despite so many modern interpretations and although it may be reasonable to avoid them on organs built since 1750. On the other hand, Carl Philipp said his father understood the art of registration very well and drew stops 'in his own manner' such as 'astounded' other organists. Perhaps even more significant is Carl Philipp's further remark that the art had 'died with him'.[1]

---

[1] Letter of *c.* 1774, translated by David and Mendel, *op. cit.*, p. 276.

Calendar

Phrases in quotation marks are taken from the Obituary.

1685–1700	*i* Eisenach. *ii* Ohrdruf.
March 1700	Lüneburg. Chorister of the Michaelskirche. Said to have travelled 'occasionally' to Hamburg and to have heard Reinken there.
1703	Weimar. Received commission to test organ in the New Church, Arnstadt.
1703–7	Organist of the New Church, Arnstadt (Bonifatiuskirche). Criticised for long interludes in chorales and for too bold harmonisation. At Arnstadt 'revealed the first fruits of his industriousness in the art of organ-playing and composition'.
1705–6	Winter journey to Lübeck to hear Buxtehude.
1707–8	Organist at Divi Blasiikirche, Mühlhausen. Had the Mühlhausen organ rebuilt to his specification.
1708–17	Organist to the Court at Weimar.
1714	Weimar. Promoted to *Concertmeister*.
1716	With Kuhnau and C. F. Rolle, reported on new organ of the Liebfrauenkirche, Halle.
1717–23	Capellmeister to the Court at Cöthen.
1717	Reported on the rebuilt organ of the Paulinerkirche, Leipzig.
1720	Played to Reinken at the Katharinenkirche, Hamburg. Withdrew from candidature for organist's post at the Jakobikirche, Hamburg.
1723	'Entered upon the cantorate' at St Thomas, Leipzig.
1723	Inaugurated the small organ at Störmthal (still extant).
1731	At least third visit to Dresden, playing in public (including Sophienkirche where W. F. Bach appointed organist in 1733).
1732	Examined rebuilt organ of the Martinikirche, Kassel.
1739	*Clavierübung III* published by the author.
1746	Examined the new large organ of the Wenzelskirche, Naumburg (together with Gottfried Silbermann).
1750	Died in Leipzig, 28 July, 'mourned by all true connoisseurs of music'.
1751	*Art of Fugue* published.